Murphys Don't Quit

ADVANCE PRAISE FOR *MURPHYS DON'T QUIT*

"This story of having it all, then having to fight for it all back, is one that many of us go through in our lives to different degrees. Colleen Murphy shares a great story, delivering strength and hope through her message in *Murphys Don't Quit*! Her determination and ability to pull together the tragic pieces to provide a positive outcome for her daughter, Lauren, and her family will inspire you!"

—**Kelly Behlmann,** founder and executive director of Disabled Athlete Sports Association.

"Prepare for a powerful journey because you're about to laugh, cry, feel agony, celebrate hope, and realize not only why the *Murphys Don't Quit* in their lives, but why you shouldn't quit in yours. In difficult times, this story reminds us all that miracles still happen and the best is yet to come."

—**John O'Leary,** two-time national bestselling author and host of the *Live Inspired Podcast*

"*Murphys Don't Quit* is the gripping saga of a survivor's setbacks and triumphs over traumatic brain injury, but it goes far beyond your typical inspirational memoir. Meet Lauren Murphy, and you'll quickly understand how she attracted a legion of fans, including an endlessly devoted family, loyal friends, and even a few *A*-list celebrities after a tragic accident left her unable to walk or talk. With relentless hope, honesty, and her trademark humor, Colleen Murphy tells the story of raising her daughter twice—while finding blessings in the second chance she never wanted. The Murphy family teaches us to never quit pushing, never quit fighting, and most importantly, never quit on each other."

—**Blythe Bernhard,** St. Louis Post-Dispatch

"*Murphys Don't Quit* is a masterpiece. What makes it so is its universality. It's not another "head injury" book. It's a gut-level, honest account of how to love with everything you are."

—**Sarah Davis**, CBIST, The Brain Injury Foundation of St. Louis

"A must read for families facing adversity when calamity strikes. Readers will find comfort, inspiration —and most importantly—HOPE!"

—**Carol Dow-Richards,** director, Aphasia Recovery Connection

"Colleen Murphy has given us all a gift, a guide to maintaining hope when life gives us our worst moments. The inspiring story of a devastating injury, an indefatigable spirit, a family's faith, and the power of never giving up will give you the keys to land on hope no matter what happens in your life. Lauren, Colleen, and their family's motto is 'Murphys Don't Quit.' That's a great lesson for us all."

—**W. Lee Warren, MD,** author of *I've Seen the End of You: A Neurosurgeon's Look at Faith, Doubt, and the Things We Think We Know* and host of The Dr. Lee Warren Podcast

"*Murphys Don't Quit* takes us on an emotional journey through the heart of a mother and the mind of a brain injury survivor. After receiving the call that every mother dreads, Colleen Murphy boards a plane to California beginning an epic battle she never wanted to fight, with a ferocity she never knew she had. Murphy masterfully weaves raw pain with quick wit leaving readers laughing on one page and crying on the next. Beyond its' message of hope and unbreakable spirits, *Murphys Don't Quit* provides an often-neglected perspective of a family effected by brain injury. This memoir should be required reading for all health care professionals and anyone questioning the healing power of love, laughter, family, and perseverance."

—**Amanda Eaton, PhD, CCC-SLP**

"Murphy's telling of this story is honest, quirky, touching, inspiring, and - at times - sarcastic and irreverent. She aptly conveys the weight of numerous challenges that Lauren has faced due to her traumatic brain injury, and provides rich examples of how associated hardships are experienced by the entire family and others whose lives intersect with Lauren's. The reader is invited into intimate, complex, and sometimes raw details about relationships among members of the whole Murphy family, including the struggles and triumphs of a marriage affected profoundly by Lauren's injury. *Murphys Don't Quit* is a testimony to important facts: recovery can continue for many years; sustained support from family, friends, and community is absolutely vital; having someone commit to helping find and secure the best professional help is invaluable; and humor is healing. This story is also an affirmation of persistence, hard work, love, faith, and hope. The summary of Lauren's lessons learned through recovery are wonderful reminders to all of us."

—Brooke Hallowell, PhD, CCC-SLP

MURPHYS DON'T QUIT

5 Keys to Unlocking Hope
When Life Seems Hopeless

COLLEEN MURPHY

NEW YORK

LONDON • NASHVILLE • MELBOURNE • VANCOUVER

Murphys Don't Quit

5 Keys to Unlocking Hope When Life Seems Hopeless

Published in New York, New York, by Morgan James Publishing. Morgan James is a trademark of Morgan James, LLC. www.MorganJamesPublishing.com

Morgan James BOGO™

A **FREE** ebook edition is available for you or a friend with the purchase of this print book.

CLEARLY SIGN YOUR NAME ABOVE

Instructions to claim your free ebook edition:
1. Visit MorganJamesBOGO.com
2. Sign your name CLEARLY in the space above
3. Complete the form and submit a photo of this entire page
4. You or your friend can download the ebook to your preferred device

ISBN 9781631955174 paperback
ISBN 9781631955181 ebook
Library of Congress Control Number:
2021931253

Cover Design by:
Lori Finklang

Interior Design by:
Christopher Kirk
www.GFSstudio.com

NOTE TO THE READER

This work is a memoir. It reflects the author's present recollection of her experiences over a period of years. Certain names, locations, and identifying characteristics have been changed. Dialogue and events have been recreated from memory, and, in some cases, have been compressed to convey the substance of what was said or what occurred. Some scenes are composites of events, and the time line for some events has been compressed.

Morgan James is a proud partner of Habitat for Humanity Peninsula and Greater Williamsburg. Partners in building since 2006.

Get involved today! Visit
MorganJamesPublishing.com/giving-back

To my current and future sons-in-law, I'm sorry they are all so crazy.
To my future-daughter-in-law, run!

CONTENTS

ACKNOWLEDGMENTS

"Raising kids is like trying to nail Jell-O to a tree."
—Unknown

Thank you to Amanda Eaton, Mary Weinman, and Kelsey and Maggie Murphy for reading my early chapters. You girls gave me the confidence to keep going.

To my editor, Patrick Price you are brilliant; thanks for believing in me.

To Mom, thanks for always being my number one cheerleader. Because of you, I knew how to be a good mom. Even when money was tight, I had name brand shoes and Jordache Jeans. Sorry I was such a brat!

To Dad, thank you for showing me how to find humor in everything. Only the good die young. I miss you!

David Murphy, you complete me. I couldn't do any of this craziness without you. I appreciate and love you more than you will ever know. Thank you for your unwavering love and support.

To Sam, you are one of my greatest gifts. Thanks for being such a positive role model for all the littles.

To Lauren, thanks for finding your way back to me. You amaze me every single day.

To Erin, you will always be my little Kooks. I'm thankful you stopped biting people.

To Shannon, underneath your brutal honesty lies one of the kindest souls around. Gingers *do* have souls.

To Kelsey, your confidence and boldness will lead you to great things. Never lose your sense of adventure. Keep being you.

To Ryan, you are one of the funniest humans on the planet. You were worth the wait. Please stop crashing my cars.

To Maggie, you were the final piece of the puzzle; you made our family complete. Thanks for being the chillest girl I know.

To the Murphy safety net: (too many people to list). You know who you are. Your help during our time of need did not go unnoticed. Every single act of kindness was felt and appreciated.

To all current and future brain injury families, you have my heart. I hope this book gives you a laugh or two and helps you understand that no matter how hard it is to face each day, the next day will always be better. Hold on!

Chapter One

THE CALL

I vaguely remember boarding the plane. The little boy seated behind me was bursting with joy over his upcoming visit to Disneyland. The energy floating around my row was vastly different from what I was experiencing. I spent the duration of the flight ineffectively trying to hold back the flood of tears covering my grief-stricken face.

When I had woken that morning, I had no idea I would be spending my Friday night on a crowded flight paralyzed with fear. I passed the time by begging God to put me out of my misery. I actually preferred dying in a fiery plane crash to landing safely, driving to Cedars Sinai Hospital, and watching one of my children die.

———

St. Louis, Missouri, on Friday, April 19, 2013, was dark and dreary. I was thrilled to reach the end of a stressful workweek. Spring was nowhere in sight, the sun was hiding yet again, as it had been for all of April. I recently gave myself a Web MD diagnosis of *seasonal affective disorder.* My guess is that doctors came up with this ailment for people like me just looking for a good excuse to be a royal witch. The grass was brown, the trees still bare; the air was damp and cold. This forty-three-year-old, slightly wrinkled sun-worshipper had been in a bad mood for quite a while.

Earlier in the week, I optimistically brought all my spring/summer clothes out of storage in the hopes that it might help the weather change course. I also prayed that my summer clothes still fit, as that was becoming an issue with each passing year. My metabolism came to a screeching halt around my fortieth birthday. *Yay me!* Ignoring all the anticipated (yet still too thin) spring dresses in my closet, that morning I'd picked yet another dull winter outfit—gray dress pants (a little tight in the waist) and a Crest toothpaste-colored, long-sleeved top—it matched the mood of the day. At least I got to wear my favorite comfy black flats from Target; I had worn them so often that there were visible holes in the soles of both shoes. I was always careful in business meetings not to cross my legs in case someone would notice their condition. I knew I would have to throw them away eventually but today was not the day.

I had no clue I would be wearing that ugly outfit for the next five days.

My workday ended a little early so I would have time to watch my daughter Kelsey's high school soccer game. Before merging onto the highway, I clicked on a Facebook video advertising an upcoming Rick Springfield fans getaway at Club Med. Obviously, I shouldn't have been paying any attention to the video while driving, but when it came to my teenage crush, I tended to break all the rules. As a kid, I used all of my babysitting earnings to buy *Tiger Beat* magazines featuring photos of Rick. My childhood bedroom was decorated in wall-to-wall Rick. He was my very first boyfriend—technically my first imaginary boyfriend. The obsession was so strong that I can't reflect on my childhood without thinking of Rick. I had an awesome imagination, or I was just a raving lunatic. Maybe a combination of both? Rick was a terrible kisser. Yes, I never *actually* kissed him, but I knew without a doubt that his poster version of himself was a lousy kisser.

A call came through, interrupting my cell phone video. The caller ID read "Private Number."

Looking back, I wish I would have thrown my phone out the window instead. Not answering the phone wouldn't have changed the events of the day, but in my head, everything bad in my life can be directly linked to that dreadful call.

Before the call, life was good. My marriage was strong. My kids (all seven of them) were growing up to be amazing, kind, and loving people. I had a job that I loved (after spending almost twenty years as a stay-at-home mom). Financially, we were finally in a place where paying bills wasn't a constant struggle. Dealing with moody kids, an occasionally grumpy husband, carpools, girl drama (I have six daughters), and boy drama, (I have only one son, yet often feels like six) was what made life seem hard. Our biggest problem in life was that our dog Seamus peed on anything and everything unless he was outside. Outdoors, he didn't know what to do; he couldn't find a chair or a couch to pee on. We had to put him in doggy diapers and his veterinarian prescribed Prozac. I was waiting patiently for Seamus's antidepressant to take effect.

"Hello," I said to the mystery caller.

The voice on the other end identified himself as a Los Angeles detective. My heart intuitively sank. He then asked how I was related to Lauren Murphy. I nervously told him that I was her mother. It's amazing how many scenarios flew through my head. *Is she in jail? Is she too busy to call me herself? Was she the victim of a crime?* I could not for the life of me figure out why a detective was calling me.

Lauren lived in New York City. She moved there after a bad breakup. She was gutsy and knew exactly what she wanted and how to get it. I missed having her in St. Louis but loved to visit her in New York. I was proud of her independence and the life she was creating for herself. She recently landed an exciting new job and was currently on a business trip in . . . Los Angeles. In fact, I had talked to her early that morning. It was the week after the Boston Marathon bombing. Police were closing in on a suspect and the city of Boston was on lockdown. Lauren's new boyfriend was originally from Boston. I'd called her to ask if his family had been affected by the police search. I forgot about the two-hour time difference and woke her up. We chatted for a while until I lost service pulling into a parking garage.

Once I identified myself as Lauren's mother, the detective informed me that Lauren had been involved in an accident. She was hit by a car while out running. My head started spinning, thoughts going too fast for my brain to comprehend. *Why didn't she call me?* I thought. *She is probably annoyed that it will put a damper in her marathon training.* She had just been accepted into the New York City Marathon and was super excited. Within two seconds I snapped out of it, realizing how serious this must be. My palms on the steering wheel were sweating, and my heart seemed to be beating right out of my chest.

"Does she have head trauma?" I asked the detective.

"No," he replied, but he believed she might have some internal injuries. He offered the phone number of a person at the hospital that could give me more information. I needed to pull over to write the information down. I'd already passed three exits; I could not figure out how to get off the stupid highway. I was so distraught I couldn't even function. This extra time allowed more awkward chit-chat while panic settled in.

"Take your time," the detective said, "It's okay; go slow. I can wait. Be safe."

Finally, I found an exit and pulled into a random parking lot. I jotted down the phone number and thanked the patient detective for the information. My life had just gone into a tailspin, but at least I still had good manners.

When I hung up, the Rick Springfield video resumed playing, as if my life hadn't been shattered. I was so annoyed—how empty and shallow I felt seeing that video. Five minutes ago, I had been feeling sorry for myself because I couldn't be a groupie due to work and family commitments. I wished that still mattered. What a difference five minutes can make.

I tried to call my husband, Dave, but he didn't answer. I did not leave a message. I said a quick Hail Mary and punched in the number for the hospital social worker. She answered on the first ring.

After identifying myself, the first thing I asked was, "Does she have head trauma?" Looking back it's crazy how I already knew the truth, even though the detective had just assured me that she didn't.

"I'm sorry," the social worker responded, "yes, she has severe head trauma."

I choked back tears as I asked if Lauren was going to die.

"If you are asking me if you need to come, the answer is yes."

I knew by her tone that I had to get to my girl as fast as I could.

Lauren had been a Jane Doe for several hours before they were able to identify her. I thought of my baby lying there fighting for her life, a face without a name. Her name in the hospital system was Trauma Foxtrot 5395. Did the people caring for her know how loved Trauma Foxtrot was and how much we all desperately needed her to live? I let the social worker know we would be on the first plane we could find.

I called Dave back and thankfully this time he answered. After tearfully explaining what happened, I asked him to get us on the quickest flight out of

Lambert Airport. I had about a forty-minute drive home. Luckily my ability to take charge switched to autopilot. I had several more important calls to make to be sure all of my kids and closest family members were notified. With such a large family, I needed to reach a few key people and delegate the daunting task of letting others know.

After first trying to reach my oldest daughter Sam, I called the next oldest (after Lauren). At twenty-one, Erin was away at school in Mobile, Alabama. She was just finishing her shift at nursing clinicals when she answered my call. Next, I called my mom, who lives with us, to let her know and asked her to tell Ryan and Maggie, my two youngest kids. Maggie had a slumber birthday party that night for a classmate. As usual, I hadn't even bought the gift. *Was I seriously chastising my parenting and thinking about birthday gifts?* With the soccer game, I knew that Kelsey was my only daughter I wouldn't be able to reach before we left for the airport. I reached my friend Jill, whose daughter was Kelsey's best friend and played on the same soccer team. I knew Jill was the right call to make as someone who could gently deliver the news. Otherwise, I was afraid Kelsey would see something on Facebook or Twitter before someone could reach her. Erin was ultimately able to reach Sam, as well as her sister Shannon, who was also away at college. I hated that I wasn't able to sit each one of my children down and explain to them what happened in person. There just wasn't any time; I was desperate to get to LA as quickly as possible.

Driving home, I wasn't even sure how I kept my car between the white lines. I guess it was from all the practice I had watching Rick Springfield videos instead of the road?

Lauren's brain surgeon, Dr. Chen, called as I was merging onto the final highway that leads to our home. He let me know that he had been monitoring Lauren all day. They had drilled holes in her skull in the ER to try and alleviate the pressure.

Did he just tell me he *drilled holes* in Lauren's head?

The trauma was so severe that they needed to do more for Lauren to stand a chance at survival. I knew it was bad, and I was absolutely terrified. The plan was to take her back to surgery and remove a portion of her skull. This would give her brain room to swell. Fun fact: they don't need consent in severe cases when the family can't be reached. There is a policy in place where two doctors can sign off on the surgery as emergent and necessary. It was just a bonus that the police had been able to identify her before surgery. Dr. Chen carefully explained things to me, his voice kind and compassionate. I have no idea what I said to him or how I reacted, the events of the previous fifteen or twenty minutes were still part of a world that I was desperately hoping wasn't real. Somehow, I made it home in one piece and had about an hour before we had to leave for the airport.

Inside my house, I tried to keep a brave face. Ryan and Maggie were only thirteen and eleven. I didn't want to scare them. I began packing clothes, though I had no clue how long I would be gone, what I would need, or if Lauren would even be alive when I got there. I sat at our kitchen table with my head in my hands sobbing. There was nothing else I could do. I felt so helpless, I could barely even hold my head up.

My little Maggie walked up to me and gave me a hug. Her face looked so sad. *I* was always the strong one, who rarely got upset. Sure, I often screamed like a banshee over messy rooms, but *crying* wasn't in my wheelhouse. Raging lunatic, yes. Emotional cripple, no! Regrettably, I completely crumbled. I will never forget the look on Maggie's face. I felt as if I had failed her on so many levels. Mothers are supposed to shield their children from pain, not add to it. Even in times of desperation, a mother's guilt still rears its ugly head.

The ride to the airport was tense, the silence deafening with the exception of my soft whimpering in the backseat. Rarely am I ever in a car without sound. The radio at least is always playing in the background. But today wasn't a day for music. And there were no words that could have made any of us feel better, so we sat in silence. I glanced at the many texts coming through, yet I couldn't even respond or fully grasp what was happening. Why *my* family?

I don't remember checking our luggage at the airport, getting our boarding passes, or going through security. I do remember sitting on an uncomfortable plastic chair, anxiously waiting to board the plane, my face slick with a torrential downpour of never-ending salty tears. Dave was fielding phone calls from friends and family as I sat in a nearly catatonic trance.

A call from Dr. Chen went straight to voicemail. Seeing the missed call, I found a quiet spot against a wall in between two digital signs to listen to the voice-mail. Dr. Chen's message was vague. Lauren made it through surgery and he left a number to call for further details. I called the number, hoping to reach Lauren's surgeon. Instead, I was connected to her ICU nurse, John, who had been assigned to Lauren after her surgery. He had a soft and sincere voice; I liked him immediately. He came across as the kind of caring man you would want on your team.

John had the unlucky task of conveying the not-so-great news on behalf of Dr. Chen. He started with the positive fact that Lauren's vitals were good, then the list of bad news seemed to go on forever. Lauren was in a coma, receiving blood transfusions, and her brain was continuing to swell. The swelling was the area of greatest concern and was expected to get worse over the next three to four days. Lauren had been brought to the neuro ICU and was being monitored closely. John also reported that instead of taking a small section of her skull behind her ear as planned, they had to remove a rather large section on the left side of her skull. The original plan was to surgically implant the skull piece into her stomach so it would remain nourished, sterile, and healthy for reattachment later. But because of multiple fractures, they were unable to save the removed piece of skull. It was a problem that would need to be addressed at a later date. *Did he just say that she is missing parts of her skull and they aren't able to replace it later?* My head was spinning again, as I took in all of the information. I thought to myself, *why in the world didn't I bring a pen and paper with me before I called the hospital?* I'm not sure what I was expecting. I guess something along the lines of: "Surgery went well; she is resting comfortably." Or better yet, "I'm sorry Mrs. Murphy, there has been a crazy mix-up. Trauma Foxtrot 5395 belongs to someone else. Your daughter is at her scheduled work event, killing it, per usual."

Instead, I heard the worst possible news ever. "Her damage was so extensive they had to perform a lobectomy on her left temporal lobe."

I had no idea what that even meant, but I could tell by his tone it didn't mean anything good. I asked for clarity and John let out an audible sigh. I knew I was going to hear something terrible. John explained that a lobectomy was when a portion of the brain is removed. I was so confused; I had never heard of someone missing part of their brain. I asked Nurse John if she would ever be able to live a normal life? After a longer than normal pause, he responded, "I don't know."

I wanted to die right that second. I seriously did not want to be amongst the living and breathing. My daughter was in trouble and there wasn't a darn thing I could do about it. I hung up the phone and all I wanted to do was lie in the fetal position in the middle of Lambert Airport. Instead, I pulled myself together, went back over to our seats, and let Dave know the grim update. The word "grief" took on a whole new meaning.

How could I fix this? I was her *mother*, somehow this had to be my fault. I begged and pleaded with God. Was I being punished for not being a good enough person? I tried to be a good Catholic. I went to Mass every Sunday, put all of my kids through Catholic school (even when we couldn't afford it), raised all my kids to know God and to love Jesus. Why was this happening? Obviously, I wasn't good enough, wasn't mother enough, wasn't wife enough, wasn't Christian enough—I had to be punished.

Once on the plane, I was full of anxiety. We had to fly to Chicago first for a short layover before we headed to LAX. Once we were at Midway Airport in Chicago, I wanted to make sure my phone was fully charged in case the hospital tried to call again. In the terminal, I found a small cramped charging station. I was standing shoulder to shoulder amongst half a dozen other travelers charging their phones or tablets when my phone rang.

It was another "Private Number." I didn't have much luck with the last private number, yet I didn't have much to lose, so I answered. On the other end was Father Joe, my parish priest. Someone must have called him after hearing about the accident. I tearfully explained all from the beginning. By the time I got to the part where they removed part of Lauren's brain, my sobs were becoming louder and louder. I noticed the people standing closest to me awkwardly trying to avoid eye contact, they couldn't help but overhear my whole conversation. Father Joe asked if we could pray together and, of course, I obliged. I can't recollect if we prayed an "Our Father" or a "Hail Mary" or both, but I do remember feeling comfort in his words and assurance that he would continue to pray for us. I'm pretty sure if my neighbors at the phone charging station could have hightailed it out of there without coming across as rude, they would have run away as if the building were on fire.

Soon after, we boarded the plane. Buying tickets a few hours before takeoff equals "C" group and back of the plane. We ended up in the second to last row. At the final row behind us sat a mother and her two kids, the dad was in the window seat in our row. The kids were headed to Disneyland in the morning and could barely control their excitement. Their little boy seemed to be around four years old and was completely over the moon. He kept loudly talking to his dad who was to my left.

Desperate for hospital updates, I had brought my laptop and was connected to Wi-Fi. I had given Nurse John verbal permission to talk to Sam on our behalf with any updates on Lauren's condition. Sam was at home taking care of her siblings and calling the hospital every hour, on the hour. She emailed me any news she could get her hands on.

The closer we came to land, the sicker I felt; I was so scared. Up until this point, I could pretend this was all part of a bad dream. Once I got to the hospital, there would be no turning back, no second-guessing what had really happened. I can only assume the stranger next to me was cursing himself due to his stellar seat selection skills. The blubbering mess to his right was most likely not what he bargained for. I had yet to perfect the silent cry.

We arrived in LA a little after midnight—2:00 a.m. St. Louis time—and the airport was largely deserted. Lucky for me, Dave had been to LAX recently and knew his way around. I don't think I had the mental capacity to find the baggage claim area regardless of the many overhead signs leading the way. We collected our bags then headed toward rental cars. Dave traveled often for work and was part of the reward club. Reward members were offered picks of the aisle. Unfortunately, the only car left in the aisle after midnight was a two-door Dodge Challenger, so off we went to the hospital in a sports car, looking like we were in the middle of a mid-life crisis versus a catastrophic, real-life crisis.

There was more silence as Google Maps directed us toward Cedars-Sinai. Fear had taken hold and wasn't letting go. Thirty minutes later we arrived at the hospital complex with no clue where to go. Luckily the charge nurse had asked us to call when we arrived, and she would come down and meet us.

We walked into the lobby attached to the garage and there wasn't a person in sight. I called the charge nurse to let her know we were in the lobby; her voice was full of warmth and I knew that she was another person that I would grow to love. A few minutes later, she called back looking for us, and after a few questions, we learned we were in the wrong lobby. We stood in a new building that hadn't even opened yet, hence the ghost town. She asked me to stay put, as we both agreed it would be easier for her to come to us. Ten minutes later I spotted a woman in scrubs holding a bulky phone headed our way. I took in her warm inviting smile, then noticed her unusual hairstyle. As a former hairstylist, I had never seen anything like it. Hairstyles in the Midwest were obviously way different than hairstyles on the West Coast. She sported an unusually tall afro. To say it was unique was a huge understatement. It looked as if she woke up every morning, slapped on some product, and designed her hairstyle to mimic an abstract sculpture, highlighting several triangular-shaped sections. I thought to myself, *Dorothy, you aren't in Kansas anymore.* Or in my case, Missouri.

We continued awkward chit-chat (it was becoming a skill) as we worked our way through the huge hospital complex. There are excellent hospitals in St. Louis. One of them covers several city blocks. But this was different. The complex was *massive.* We would have never found our way alone. I was very thankful she came down to get us. She mentioned that we were headed to the Saperstein Critical Care Tower and I let that name sink in a bit. It sounded almost Disney-like, only Lauren wasn't a captive Rapunzel and I wasn't a handsome prince coming to rescue her. This tower was for critical patients.

I hated that tower before we even arrived.

We eventually found ourselves standing in the lobby of the Saperstein Critical Care Tower. In the corner of the room, a man sat behind a computer at a little desk. I found it odd that they had an employee sitting there after midnight. He looked at us kind of strange—I guess because of the hour, or maybe the unique hairstyle? The nurse let him know we were the parents of Trauma Foxtrot and he nodded in a sympathetic way. I wanted to curl up in a ball and die. Her name is *not* Trauma Foxtrot; it is Lauren Murphy, born on October 5, 1987, at 4:11 a.m., 7 lbs., 8 oz., twenty-two inches long, arriving after twenty-two hours of labor!

When Lauren was born, she had an APGAR score of 3—all new babies receive an APGAR score based on their health at birth. The assessments are done at one minute after birth and again at five minutes. I would bet most people don't even know that this test exists (unless their child was in the abnormal range like mine). I had a very difficult, long labor. When Lauren was born, she had trouble breathing and it took her a long time to *pink up* as they say. A former teacher of hers shared with me once at a parent-teacher conference that Lauren liked to share in class that she was born purple. She loved it when I would tell her the story of her birth.

I will never forget how scared I was as a brand-new mom; I was so happy to have finally delivered Lauren and then my happiness quickly turned to fear. She underwent a spinal tap moments after birth because doctors feared she had meningitis. Thankfully they were wrong, and she just had some extra fluid in her lungs. She would be fine with a short stay in the NICU, a little oxygen, and some antibiotics. Lauren was a fighter back then and I was counting on her to be a fighter now. I remember being afraid to see Lauren in the NICU. A friend of mine wheeled me in to see her because my legs were still numb from the epidural. Next to the other babies, Lauren looked so big. Most of the other babies in the NICU were premature. She had a clear cake plate-looking thing over her head that was supplying oxygen, her blond curls were still wet from delivery. She was finally all pink and soft and warm. I reached my hand into the bassinet and she wrapped her sweet little hand around my index finger. I never felt a love so strong in my life. I had no idea that my heart was even capable of this kind of love. I made a promise to God in that very instant that I would devote my whole life to this beautiful baby girl. Now I stood here in this lobby silently pleading with God to please not take my baby away from me.

I needed these doctors to be wrong just like they were when she was born.

Inside the sterile box of an elevator, I knew there would be no turning back. I braced myself for what I would be seeing in just a few moments. We were headed up to the eighth floor, my mouth suddenly dry and my legs beginning to buckle.

But first, we stopped on the second floor. The doors opened and a few seconds later they closed. There was not a soul in sight. Did someone change their mind? The charge nurse explained that Cedars-Sinai is a Jewish hospital, and since it was after midnight, it was technically Saturday, the Sabbath—a day of rest, and pushing an elevator button is considered work. *What?* I am not one to knock religion, especially one so old and deeply rooted in tradition like Catholicism, but seriously? You can't push a button? All I wanted was to get to my daughter and now I had to torturously stop on each and every level until we reached the eighth floor. It would have been comical in a different situation. There I was with a nurse who had hair taller than my legs in an elevator with a door that would open and close a total of fifteen times before I could reach my destination. Only it wasn't funny—today would be a day without laughter. Today was my darkest day ever. Technically *yesterday* was my darkest day. I wasn't quite sure what today would be, but my best guess was that it wouldn't be good.

Little did I know that the coming days would make the dark, dreary month of April seem like I had been walking on sunshine. The darkness that would consume my next several weeks and months was something I could not have even begun to fathom.

Chapter Two

ICU

Nurse Crazy Hair explained that Lauren would look very different. She was doing her best to prepare us. As we passed the neuro ICU's nursing station, I could feel all eyes on us. Many of the staff immediately stopped what they were doing and watched us with sorrow and compassion. I sensed that each and every one of them knew that once we walked through the threshold of Lauren's ICU room, our lives would never be the same.

Lauren's room was down a long hall, second to last on the left. Nurse Becky was there waiting for us. As I stepped inside, it felt like walking in quicksand. Though only a few steps away from my daughter, it seemed like an eternity before I finally reached her bedside.

I hardly recognized her. This battered, bruised lifeless body couldn't possibly be my Lauren. Wearing a green and purple diamond patterned hospital gown, she was positioned with her head all the way at the very top of the bed. Just below her bottom lip, reaching to her mid-chest area, was a large cervical collar. I didn't know if or where I should touch her.

Becky explained to me that the collar was there to keep her still until they were able to confirm with absolute certainty that she did not have any spinal injuries. To me, it looked as if the collar was swallowing her little body whole. There were stark white pillows positioned under each arm, pushing her upper limbs in a downward V shape toward the edge of the bed. The pillows overlapped both sides of her body, making her small torso appear to be half its width. Looking at her this way reminded me of when she was around age four.

Lauren was always a tiny little girl with a mound of thick strawberry blond curls. Brushing her curls only made them seem to grow larger; it was best to just let them be. Even as an adult, she often commented on how hard it was to "tame her mane." Her present state was in cold stark contrast to those beautiful bouncy curls. Lauren's head was wrapped in a white bandage: on the right side, a matted mess of blood-stained hair poked out the top; the left side was blood soaked and you could see that her head had been shaved. There was dried blood on the inside of her left ear, cascading down her neck.

In blue writing on a piece of medical tape, the top of her bandage read: NO BONE FLAP. That was to remind others that she could not have her head positioned on that side due to her missing skull. A sign above her bed broadcast the same reminder.

No bone flap.

The areas of her face that remained visible beneath the various pieces of medical equipment were full of bruising. Her beautiful blue eyes were deeply hidden beneath dark purple swollen eyelids. The swelling on her eyes was so bad it looked as if she had two golf balls stuffed under her eyelids. Lauren's hands were tied to the bed. Becky explained that it was just a precaution to make sure she didn't try and pull off any of her tubes and or monitors. Her left arm was wrapped with a blood pressure cuff and both of her legs were wrapped in air compression leg cuffs. Her body was holding on to so much fluid that every inch of her was swollen. Her hands, although perfectly manicured, looked like they belonged to someone else.

The only part of her that looked remotely familiar was her nose. Her perfectly shaped, lightly freckled, petite, little nose. I tried to center my focus on her nose. I knew she was still in there and she was facing the fight of her life.

The right side of her room held several different types of monitors. The lights and numbers on each machine looked complicated and terrifying. She was connected to several pieces of tubing and IVs. Her mouth was in an open position, her top teeth exposed. A green plastic plug was positioned between her teeth to protect the many tubes down her throat, as well as protecting her teeth. Seeing those beautiful white teeth reminded me of how often she liked to whiten them.

Back in high school, Lauren had once fallen asleep wearing her Crest White strips. The next day at school she had to wear her turtleneck over her mouth as she went from building to building changing classes because it was wintertime and the cold air caused extreme sensitivity. The things she did for beauty always gave me a good laugh, especially because she was already so naturally beautiful.

Between her upper lip and nose sat another hard-plastic piece that connected two brown pads that rested across her cheekbones secured by an elastic band wrapped around the back of her head. These pads reminded me of cushioned insoles for high heels—only these pads were being used to keep my daughter *alive* by connecting her life support machine. Large plastic tubing connected to the tubes in her mouth and veered off into two more tubes resembling a vacuum hose, forcing air into Lauren's lungs, keeping her with us. I would grow to detest this machine's unnatural rhythm as the sound switched from sending air in and bringing air out.

Even as a child, Lauren had an old soul. She was the type of kid that always hung out at the adult table and could follow and jump into an adult conversation with great confidence and poise. At four years old, her love of press-on nails, clip-on earrings, purses, and plastic high heel dress-up shoes began to take shape. Lauren was also my little cuddle bug. Even at four, she would let me scoop her up and carry her around as if she was a toddler. Once Erin was born, she lost her spot as the baby of the family, but she never gave up her spot as my cuddle bug. As an adult, she and Shannon often fought over who would rest her head in my lap to have her scalp scratched. What I wouldn't do to have a chance to lay her head in my lap right now, scratch her head, and tell her everything was going to be okay. There was nowhere I could even touch my daughter without feeling as if I would cause her more pain. I was at a compete loss, all I could do was stand there helpless.

The resident on call arrived. I'm sure this is a part of the job that doctors dread. We quickly learned that not all neurosurgeons are warm and fuzzy. This guy was young, tall and thin with dark hair. He wore navy scrubs and a white lab coat. When he entered Lauren's room, I didn't get that feeling of warmth like I did when I spoke with Dr. Chen, Nurse John, and Nurse Crazy Hair; he was different. As he began to speak, I watched the color immediately drain from my husband's face, his knees were giving out. The reality of the situation had just hit him like a freight train. Thankfully there was a chair nearby to catch him, he slid into the seat and somehow managed to remain upright as the doctor gave us the rest of the bad news. He delivered this news in a very matter-of-fact, monotone tone. Lauren's ICPs (inter-cranial pressure) were in the extremely dangerous zones and her numbers would be getting worse before they would get better. His next statement was even tougher to hear.

"If she lives, you are looking at months and months of recovery, possibly years."

It wasn't the recovery part that was hard to hear—it was the word *if.*

After that, the resident stood there in silence. It was painfully obvious he didn't know what else to say. As Dave and I tried to process everything we had just learned in the last ten minutes, he stood there awkwardly. There was so much to take in—the sounds of the machines, the sight of our battered and bruised daughter, the possibility of losing her, not to mention all the unanswered questions that we were too afraid to ask.

As the resident eventually turned to leave, he offered us something else to ponder. "Your daughter is the sickest patient in the whole hospital."

Even after he left, those words lingered in the room for what felt like an eternity. Poor Nurse Becky was stuck being the one to try and give us a shred of hope. She continued to explain all the monitors and their functions, I don't think I comprehended anything she was trying to tell us, as I was still focused on the eloquent words of Dr. Gloom and Doom. Like seriously, "The sickest person in the *whole hospital?*" I called BS. I wanted to go door to door in this vast complex so I could prove him wrong. It might take me several days to reach every single patient, but surely there had to be *someone* who was in worse shape than my kid.

Becky stayed with us all night. I took great comfort knowing she was caring for Lauren. She made me feel safe. When Lauren's ICP levels kept spiking, Nurse Becky asked the doctor on call to order a drug called Mannitol. This medication is known to aide with swelling. It removes sodium out of the brain. The neuro doctor on call (not the surgeon, another resident) refused Becky's request. He claimed the side effects associated with the severity of Lauren's injury made it too risky. Becky didn't take no for an answer; she went over his head and paged the attending physician. Fifteen minutes later, Becky was administering Mannitol. I watched as Lauren's numbers leveled out. They were still dangerously high, but at least they weren't climbing.

It was explained to us early on why the ICP numbers were so important. If her brain continued to swell, there was a good chance her brain would have nowhere to go except towards her spinal column. If that happened, it would cause her brain stem to herniate and she would be brain dead. The severity of Lauren's injury and brain swelling carried a very high risk of brain stem herniation, so Becky was with her at all times. Lauren was her only patient. Every fifteen minutes Becky would do a neuro check, first checking her pupils. All of my prior binge watching of *Grey's Anatomy* and *ER* had taught me that if her pupil was blown, she had brain stem herniation. I paid very close attention to Becky's facial expression and body language every time she shone the flashlight in Lauren's eyes. She also checked to see if Lauren would respond to pain. This was done by pinching her in the fatty part next to her armpit. Lauren's body didn't respond on the right side; pinch after pinch she laid there motionless. On the left side, Lauren's body *would* move, but not a normal type of movement. It was more like a reflex, nothing purposeful. These repeated neuro checks were hard to watch.

We spent that first night (technically morning) almost catatonic; we were shell-shocked. Nurse John took over for Becky at shift change. He was even more warm and inviting in person. I was happy John was her nurse again. I was standing just outside Lauren's room when I first met Dr. Jay Chen, her brain surgeon. I will never forget his kindness or his words of hope that morning.

"Right now, I am looking for something positive to give you," he said. "I am going to dig really deep. The positives are there; we just have to keep looking for them until we find them."

I was thankful for that simple statement. He was telling me things were really bleak, but my time would be better served focusing on the triumphs. Besides, Dave was focusing on the rough stuff enough for both of us. We have always been a good balance.

Earlier, on the way to the airport, I realized that I forgot to pack my rosary. Lauren's company had been wonderful. Her boss, Matt had sent me several texts and been in contact with Sam back at home. He made arrangements for an

LA-based colleague named Carrie to stay with Lauren after her surgery before we arrived. Carrie also left a rosary for me in Lauren's ICU room. Looking back, I realize how hard it must have been for her to sit with Lauren (a complete stranger) as she was clinging to life by a thread. Not only did Carrie sit with Lauren that first night, she also went to Lauren's hotel room the next day, packed up all of her stuff, and brought it to us at the hospital. Dave went down to the lobby to meet her. I should have gone with him to thank her myself, but I wasn't in any state of mind to greet anyone just yet.

Lauren's condition seemed to change every hour. We were asked not to touch her because it might cause sudden changes in her heart rate, blood pressure, and ICP levels. Her brain was so damaged that a simple touch could cause her nervous system too much stress. This condition is common in brain injury and is called "storming." I hated storming; I wasn't able to touch her. I wondered how else she would know I was there.

Dave came back upstairs after meeting with Carrie and brought Lauren's purse and suitcase. I immediately unzipped her suitcase, searching for something I could hold of hers that still smelled like her. Unable to touch Lauren, I was desperate for some sort of connection to my daughter.

The first thing I noticed was half her clothes still had tags on them. *Like mother, like daughter. Obviously, you can't go on a trip without a suitcase full of new clothes.* Then I came across a pink sweater that I had seen before. Erin had spent her spring break visiting Lauren in New York a few weeks earlier. They sent me a video of the two of them dancing on the long floor mat piano in FAO Schwartz (just like Tom Hanks did in the movie *Big*). Lauren was wearing that pink sweater and can be heard on the clip saying, "Let's do ballet moves for Mom." The video ended with the two of them giggling as they hopped off the keyboard. I wondered if I would ever get to hear her giggle again. I missed the sound of her voice and especially her laugh. That pink sweater became my security blanket. I would spend hour after hour clutching it, crying into its softness, and inhaling the faint smell of Lauren's perfume.

Lauren's best friend and roommate, Courtney, arrived on Sunday. When she walked into the room, she brought a much-needed energy. She marched right up to Lauren's bed and said, "Hey Luc, we need you to wake up!"

Courtney and Lauren started a blog when they moved to New York. Their blog *Life of the Lucys* had a large following. They blogged about their dates, their jobs, and basically figuring out life in the big city. Lauren was Lucy with a capital "L" and Courtney was luCy with a capital "C." I'm not sure how they started calling each other Lucy—most likely an inside joke not meant for my ears.

Now that we had Lauren's purse, the hospital was able to scan her ID and print off a bracelet with her real name. So long "Trauma Foxtrot 5395." Courtney quickly got a pen and wrote "Lucy" under Lauren's name. With Lauren's ID now scanned into her chart (it was a really good picture), staff could see how beautiful Lauren was. Nurse John came in the room and suggested we decorate the room and hang her picture on the wall. He told us how sad he felt when he saw her picture. It shouldn't matter whether or not your patient is beautiful, but for some reason it made her seem more real. It made the tragedy seem somehow more tragic. Courtney quickly got to work, making the ICU room as chic as possible. Our family has always been a bit "extra." If Lauren was going to be in the ICU fighting for her life, by God she will do it in style!

By Monday morning we were beginning to get a handle on how things worked. There was a team of neuro docs, and an entourage of nurse practitioners, residents, and interns that rounded with them every morning. Each week a different doctor was scheduled. Cedars-Sinai had three primary Neuro ICU doctors. The week Lauren arrived it was Dr. Yen who was in charge. Dr. Yen and Dr. Chen. Dr. Chen was a neurosurgeon and Dr. Yen was a neurologist. Admittedly, it was a little confusing. Both Asian, Dr. Chen was American and Dr. Yen was a first-generation immigrant. Judging by the thickness of his accent, one could only assume Dr. Yen arrived last week, I had to really strain to understand what he was saying. Dr. Yen was also not warm and fuzzy. He made Dr. Gloom and Doom seem like Suzy Sunshine. After our first experience of Dr. Yen examining Lauren, Nurse John translated for us, not only in clear English but in layman's terms.

Those first few ICU days all blurred together. I was living on Starbucks Chai Tea Lattes and very little rest. I would doze off for only a few minutes at a time in the uncomfortable vinyl recliner in the corner of the room.

Friends and family at home had been working 'round the clock to secure hotel rooms with donated points and had meals dropped off at the hospital. I didn't even want to go out to the waiting room to look at the food, much less eat it. Everyone kept telling me to eat but I couldn't; I knew that I couldn't keep anything down. I knew that it was important for me to take care of myself, but my body had been surviving on caffeine mixed with adrenaline for days. I was too afraid Lauren would die if I left her hospital room. If that happened, I would never have been able to forgive myself.

Sunday night there was a prayer service set up for Lauren at her old high school. We were able to join via FaceTime on the iPad. At first, I didn't want to be a part of it. My plan was to sit in the background and listen; I did not want to be on camera. I just couldn't face anyone yet, not even my own children. Dave had taken charge of all phone, calls, texts, and Facebook messages. I don't know what it was that made me shut down, especially in regard to my own children. My best guess is that if they asked me hard questions, I wouldn't be able to reassure them that everything was going to be okay. I didn't even know if Lauren would make it through the day.

When I heard Dave saying hi to the kids on the iPad, I knew I had to show my face. What kind of mother avoids her own children? And truthfully, it was nice to see their sweet faces. Later, a friend that had been sitting with my kids told me that seeing my face gave her great peace. She had been so heartsick for me, just seeing my face on the screen for a brief moment gave her comfort. That prayer service was a turning point for my youngest two kids. Up until that point, I don't think they were old enough to truly grasp the gravity of our situation. Seeing hundreds of people gathered in prayer for their big sister made it hard to not grasp the seriousness of Lauren's injury.

The detective who first notified me of the accident came by the hospital earlier in the week to drop off Lauren's phone (miraculously not a scratch on it). Lauren's phone had been the key factor in finding her true identity. Her phone was password protected, so the detective was unable to get to her contact list. But once Lauren started missing work appointments, someone called to look for her. The detective answered the call and was able to then obtain Lauren's emergency contact information from her employer. He also told me he doesn't get brought into traffic cases unless there is a fatality—more evidence that Lauren's life was barely hanging by a thread. Once I had her phone in my possession, I took off the case and found her hotel key and American Express Card with her name and company name right on the front. Maybe *I* should have been a detective.

On Tuesday afternoon, Courtney turned to me and said, "You stink. Go to the hotel, take a shower, brush your teeth, and change your clothes." Point taken. She assured me she would be with Lauren the whole time, and if anything changed, she would call me. As I walked out of Cedars-Sinai, the sun was blinding. I felt as if I had just emerged from hibernating. I had not been outside the hospital complex since the day we arrived. I had forgotten what fresh air and daylight felt like.

While we were at the hotel, Dave called home to check on the kids. I was still avoiding talking to them. I felt like I could barely keep my own head up, much less try and lift up the spirits of my little ones. Dave hung up after talking to our youngest, Maggie, and I asked him how she was doing.

"Maggie wants to know if Lauren is still pretty," Dave said. We both busted out laughing, the first time we had laughed in close to a week. Lauren currently looked like a cross between Rocky Dennis in the movie *Mask* and Sinead O'Conner during her tearing up the picture of the Pope era. I asked Dave what he told her.

"Yeah buddy, Lauren is still pretty."

We laughed even harder; it was good to know Dave and I hadn't lost our sick sense of humor. I am sure each one of my kids had a different way to try and process what was going on. To an eleven-year-old, knowing her sister was still pretty made her feel more secure.

It felt good to shower. The sensation of the hot water against my skin was a much-needed comfort—what a change from the cold, sterile hospital room I had been living in over the last several days. I wouldn't allow myself too much time, as I had to get back to the hospital as quickly as possible. I brushed my teeth and hair and then unzipped the bag that I had hastily packed before leaving for the airport. It felt like Friday had been a lifetime ago.

Judging by my packed options, it didn't take too much time to realize I would not be dressing to impress. Was my Crest toothpaste shirt seriously the nicest thing I had with me? What was I thinking? I obviously didn't put much thought into packing. Ultimately, I went with a pair of salmon-colored sweatpants and a black V-neck tee. Upon my return to the hospital, Courtney's unfiltered response was, "Oh Dear God, you need to burn those pants." She also let us know that Dave's plaid shorts were out of style and he needed to step up his game in regard to hair products. She had been at the hotel earlier in the day and spotted Dave's hair gel (LA Looks mega hold) on the sink. Through the insults, I was thankful for some normalcy. She wasn't telling us anything our own daughters—especially Lauren—wouldn't share.

Chapter Three

MEETING THE DRIVER

By midweek we had the ICU figured out. We knew when the team did rounds, where we could store our leftover food (nowhere), and where we could curl up on a couch for a nap in the waiting room (nowhere). Cedars-Sinai was an impressive hospital but when it came to comfort for the growing wave of visitors, I would have to give them a thumbs down. More and more of our friends and family were arriving and we were busting at the seams.

The female police officer who was first on the scene of Lauren's accident made a visit to the hospital. A nurse came to let me know that the officer was there to see me. She was waiting in a tiny back office, sitting at a table wearing her navy blue LAPD uniform and holding her police hat. She introduced herself and told me how sorry she was. As soon as she began to speak, she started crying. I wrapped my arms around her and gave her a big hug. It was clear that April 19, 2013 would be a shift that she would never forget. She asked about Lauren's present condition and let me know she had been and would continue to pray for us. The man who was driving the car that hit Lauren had been in contact with the officer. He wanted to get in touch with us but did not know how to reach us or if we would even agree to see him. I let her know that it was okay for him to reach out.

A few hours later the security desk called to let us know Matthew (the man that hit Lauren) would like to come upstairs. When the elevator doors opened, Matthew nervously walked toward us. He brought a friend along for moral support. My first emotion upon seeing him was sorrow. He was tall, thin, and appeared to be about my age. From the look of his tired eyes, we also shared the same minimal sleep schedule. He awkwardly stuck out his hand to introduce himself and said, "I am Matthew. I am so sorry. Please forgive me."

I went in for a hug instead of a handshake, and through my tears let him know there was nothing to forgive. It was an accident—a tragic accident—and it wasn't his fault. Matthew was still shaking but I could tell a huge weight had been lifted. We did not invite him to go back and see Lauren, nor did he ask. I couldn't begin to imagine the amount of courage it took for him to come and offer his apology.

Minutes later, a man and woman came off the elevator looking for "The Murphy Family." They appeared to be in their early fifties. The man explained that his daughter had been in Erin's sorority in Alabama and she told them about the accident. He was with the Los Angeles FBI. They came to extend an invitation to us for whatever we may need—a place to stay, rides to and from the airport, even the use of their extra car while we were in LA. I was blown away by their kindness.

Two other men arrived (within a ten-minute time period) looking for us. One was a witness to the accident, the other was his partner. The witness wasn't doing much talking; he appeared to still be shell-shocked. He sported the same look that Matthew the driver and Dave and I wore like a heavy shroud. The waiting room was suddenly filled with several people that were strangers to us, yet we all shared a common thread. Lauren Murphy AKA "Trauma Foxtrot 5395" had somehow changed each and every person in that room.

Matthew's friend told me that he and Matthew had a falling out several years ago and they hadn't spoken since. He got a call from Matthew on Friday after the accident. Matthew was distraught and called him because he needed a friend. I was grateful that his friend shared that story with me, and I was grateful that Matthew had a much-needed friend to help him cope. In some odd way it made me feel better that she had been hit by someone who cared so deeply.

It was also nice to finally get some answers. Several days had passed since the accident and we hadn't known many details or even had the time to think about them. The witness told us that Lauren was running pretty fast as she approached the intersection. Lauren had the right of way—the pedestrian light had been on—but the light was flashing and time was running out as she approached. She must have judged she could make it before the light turned green. Unfortunately a box truck was in the left turning lane (pulled up too far), blocking her view of oncoming traffic. The light turned green and a car approached at around 40 mph just as Lauren entered its path. Drivers coming the opposite way could see the situation unfolding and honked to try and warn her. Lauren was holding her phone, listening to music with her ear buds, and couldn't hear their warning. The driver swerved to try and avoid her, but it happened too fast. His car clipped her, causing her to fly up in the air, hit the windshield in a cartwheel type motion, and then catapult over fifteen feet before eventually landing in the middle of Hollywood Boulevard.

When I spoke with Matthew, he said several times, "She was running so fast. It was like she came out of nowhere. *I tried to stop.*" Clearly, he had been replaying this tragic scene in his mind over and over again. My heart ached for him.

I was grateful for this new information from the witnesses, but felt overwhelmed by the waiting room full of strangers. Plus I hated being away from Lauren. I excused myself and headed back to her room. Dave was more comfortable in the waiting room; he could handle the rest of the conversations without me.

Most of our time, with the exception of the first night, Dave stayed either in the waiting room or outside on the hospital complex, fielding phone calls and emails. He really struggled with sitting in the room with Lauren. When he did enter, he brought the chair from the other side of the room and turned it to face me before he sat down. It was too much for him to sit and watch Lauren's lifeless body being kept alive by machines. I understood and didn't mind; I had pretty much emotionally abandoned my six other kids. Who was I to judge?

Things were not looking good. CT scans were ordered roughly twice a day. Lauren's ICP levels were still dangerously high, and she had spiked a fever. The staff requested we come for a "conference" later that afternoon. During the conference I was seated on the left side of the long table toward the far end. I nervously sat on a hard plastic chair surrounded by the neuro ICU team led by Dr. Yen. They went over their list of concerns one by one. Lauren was in trouble; things were not headed in the right direction. I listened as they talked about the many issues they were facing in regard to her care.

I believe this was the exact moment I learned to perfect the silent cry. My vision was clouded due to the onslaught of tears welling up in my eyes. I tried to focus on the people sitting around the table, yet all I could see was a blur of white lab coats. They spoke at length and in great detail, explaining what they had already done and the things they still planned to do. Most importantly, an MRI to determine the amount of brain damage we were dealing with. Lauren wasn't stable enough to undergo an MRI in her current state. They planned to lay her flat for short periods of time to mimic an MRI position. But they were unsure as to whether her fragile body could tolerate the procedure. The only positive thing they mentioned during the meeting was that she was young. This was brought up at least half a dozen times. I did not take much comfort knowing that the only positive thing they could come up with was her birthdate. And why didn't they invite Dr. Chen to this meeting?

Once finished, Dave and I sat there in stunned silence. They asked if we had questions. We had *many* questions, but we were too terrified to ask what we didn't want to hear the answer. I finally mustered the one question that I knew needed to be asked. I had secretly hoped Dave would be the one to do it. Incredibly, I found the courage to choke out my painful question.

"Do I need to fly her siblings here to say goodbye?"

The room fell silent. Eventually someone from the team responded, "If we get to that point, we have ways to artificially prolong things."

That was not the response I was looking for. When I asked the question, all I wanted them to say was a simple no. *Is that what you are doing now?* I wanted to ask, but I didn't dare to hear the answer, so I remained silent.

I was done; I had heard enough. Would it be appropriate to shout "Class dismissed! Meeting adjourned."

Or better yet, "It's time to wake up."

Chapter Four

TAYLOR AND RICK

The time had come for us to make steps that would help Lauren in her recovery. The staff had told us that Lauren would need a tracheotomy to help her breathe and a G-tube (gastrostomy tube) placed for nourishment. They mentioned several times that this would make her look so much better, as her face would be free of tubes. I was sad because I knew how important Lauren's appearance was to her. I knew she would hate having a tracheotomy. Part of me wanted to ask if this was truly necessary, but I already knew the answer. This was life or death; there was no room for vanity in the ICU. We had to agree to the procedure if we wanted Lauren to get better.

The procedure was scheduled, then rescheduled due to fevers and setbacks. Eventually they were able to get both procedures done right in her ICU room and she did well. I was excited to see her after, especially since I was led to believe she would look so much better.

Back when Lauren was in college, she struggled with really painful periods. She was diagnosed with endometriosis. Her doctor did a laparoscopy surgery to diagnose as well as burn some of the scarring. It was decided at that point to put her on a medication to trick her body into a false state of menopause. This new medication had several bad side effects. She had spent a semester in college dealing with hot flashes and severe hormone issues. Her hot flashes were so intense she would strip down and have to lay on her bed against her cinder block wall to try and cool off. Thank God she didn't have a roommate. She would call periodically, asking me questions about menopause. I wasn't even forty yet. My response was always, "Call Grandma."

One particular side effect threw her over the edge. She called me at work hysterical. I couldn't even understand what she was trying to tell me. Once I was able to calm her down, she shared with me that she had found a spider vein on the back of her thigh. I sat at my desk at work and I tried not to giggle at her ridiculousness. I rolled my eyes and couldn't believe how extremely vain she had become. I let her know it wasn't the end of the world and she would be okay. She unequivocally disagreed with me. She called her doctor and was taken off the medication that same day. Knowing how crazy she got over a tiny spider vein, I shuddered to think how she would feel about a tracheotomy.

When I was able to go back and see her after the procedure, what I saw wasn't what I was hoping for. They were correct—the tubing and vent equipment had been removed from her face—but what I wasn't prepared for was that what still remained was swollen and fragile. Having all of those tubes removed just gave me a bird's eye view of how broken she still was. Besides, the tubes were all still there, they were just moved to her neck which now had a large hole in it. Lauren's fever continued to rise; doctors were keeping a close eye on everything. She had pneumonia, which we learned is common in ICU patients. Lauren was an athlete; the staff was optimistic that her body was strong enough to fight the infection. They had ordered cooling blankets and were giving her medications to bring down her temperature.

Back in St. Louis, Sam continued to do an excellent job juggling her siblings, our house, and what had quickly becoming the command center for all incoming and outgoing information for friends and family. Three old friends of Dave's reached out to Sam to see if it would be okay if they flew to LA to spend some time with Dave. I let Sam know that I didn't think it was a good idea right now. I wasn't thinking what was best for Dave, I was being selfish. I knew Dave would not want to hang with his friends at the hospital and I was terrified that Lauren would die and I would be all alone. Even though he wasn't normally in the ICU room, I knew he was steps away and I needed him there. Dave didn't protest my decision. He seems to always put me first, so why was it so hard for me to do the same? Dave and I made a pact early on that we had to stay on the same page and keep it together. Things were not going well and we didn't want to add to an already stressful situation by being at each other's throat.

Dave and I were so humbled that people we didn't even know were bending over backward trying to help us. People reached out to celebrities, asking to send us encouragement. We had received shout out videos from some of the members of NSYNC. Lance Bass's was the first video to arrive. My Shannon had a slight obsession with Lance beginning when she was a second grader (I was in sixth grade when I began stalking Rick—Shannon was clearly an overachiever.) Seeing Lance take the time to send well wishes to a stranger gave Shannon the strength and hope that she needed. The timing was perfect. We were completely blown away. Next, we were sent a video from Joey Fatone.

A few days later, we received word that Taylor Swift wanted to donate a large sum of money to help with flights and expenses. Dave and I were shocked that Taylor was so generous to us. Lauren is close friends with one of Taylor's relatives, Nick. He wanted to do something to help us, so he reached out to Taylor to ask if she would do a shout out video for Lauren. Once she heard the details of Lauren's accident and injury, she wanted to do more than just a video.

We are so grateful to Nick; he has always been a great friend to Lauren. Before Lauren and Courtney moved to New York, Nick told Dave and me a funny story about Lauren. She asked him if he would pay her to clean his house every week. Nick already had a cleaning lady who he loved and had no intention of replacing her. My daughter Lauren has always been persistent. Nick said that she hounded him, until he caved. He felt sorry for her after she gave him some sob story that she was working two jobs trying to save enough money for the move and was still coming up short. He reluctantly told his cleaning lady that he was trying to help a friend. We still laugh when we think of how Lauren totally played him. To hear Nick, tell the story, it went something along the lines of, "She would show up each week, eat all my food, make my bed, and take my money." Dave and I weren't surprised. I don't think Lauren even knew how to hold a mop, much less use one. Frankly I'm impressed that she actually made his bed for him.

Eventually, Dave and I had our first argument since the accident. I don't even remember what the argument was about. We had started leaving the hospital at night to get some sleep. I knew we had hit a crossroads in Lauren's recovery when earlier in the week we were driving back to the hospital and the sound of Dave chomping on an apple made we want to take the apple from him and throw it out the window. If he can't figure out the proper way to eat an apple, he doesn't deserve the right to eat one. Dave is very quirky and maintains a strict routine. When he gets out of the shower, he stands in the same spot and turns his Q-tip a certain number of times in each ear. This routine can't be rushed. Turns out even if your kid is in a coma, morning routines must be enforced. We were trying our best not to make each other crazy, but on this particular day I was beginning to feel as if I had reached the end of my rope.

Courtney left for a few days to get things straightened out back in New York. I was both mentally and physically exhausted. I let Dave know he needed to stay in the ICU room with Lauren because I needed a break. I was mad. I irrationally hated him, I hated Cedars-Sinai, I hated ICU rooms, I hated LA, I hated my life, and I hated every single person I looked at that day. I knew I needed to walk away for a bit. I headed to the now very familiar Starbucks on campus to get my usual Chai Tea Latte. I hated my butchered name on the front of my cup. Every single day they messed up my name. I am used to getting "Colleen" with one "L" or one "E" but this was different, not even close. Seriously, were there no Irish people in LA? Is Colleen *that* hard of a name?

There was an outdoor courtyard area between the buildings that connected to the Saperstein Critical Care Tower. I sat on a bench in the warm sun drinking my hot tea. I secretly hated every single human who looked happy. I contemplated telling mothers walking past with their children in strollers not to get too attached to their child because they may end up running in front of a car some day and ruining their life. I was surrounded by sunlight, but it felt as if I was covered in darkness. I felt like things were never going to get better. Every time I turned around, I heard more bad news. Doctors would tell me we needed to get Lauren's ICPs below a certain number for things to improve. We would reach that number, and then they would tell us something else that needed to happen. "She needed to respond to pain on her right side." We would cross *that* hurdle and they would tell us that although she did respond, her response was that of abnormal posturing, a sign of severe brain damage. We just couldn't win. Couldn't they give us *one small, tiny victory* on anything? I sat on that bench having my very own pity party, hating everyone and everything around me.

Dave called and interrupted my party. He was the last person I wanted to talk to at that moment. *Seriously, you can't even sit in that room for ten minutes without me? It won't kill you. Man up!* Imagine my surprise (and guilt) when Dave said, "You need to get back here. I'm not kidding, Taylor Swift is on her way to visit Lauren."

I hung up the phone, wiped the old tears off my face, pulled myself together, and headed toward the elevator.

Back in Lauren's room, things were not going well. The cooling blankets were not doing their magic and they had just requested the super-duper cooling system. This fancy cooling system consisted of gel pads that wrapped around Lauren's torso, legs, arms etc. Instead of just covering her like a blanket, these gel pads wrapped around all of her skin to lower her body temperature. It looked miserable but I was grateful that Cedars-Sinai had yet another trick up their sleeve. The monitor that showed Lauren's body temperature became my main focus.

We received a call from Taylor's people that Taylor was downstairs outside the main building. Dave went down to meet her. The first thing she said when she greeted Dave was, "You're Lauren's dad? You are so young!" This caused my husband's head to triple in size as they made their way to Saperstein. Dave mentioned to me later how crazy it was to walk with Taylor and her big body guard as he watched the reactions she garnered from shocked passerby.

Lauren's nurse that day was Bryan, who was amazing. He was young and both his arms were covered in tattoos. Bryan was very concerned about Lauren's rising temperature and stayed in the room with me to keep watch. I could be wrong, but he was also excited about the visitor who was steps away from joining us.

Taylor arrived with Dave and couldn't have been more gracious. She walked right up to Lauren and asked us if Lauren could hear her? We told her we hoped that she could, but we were uncertain. There was no awkwardness; Taylor seemed so comfortable. She inquired about Lauren's current state and told us how sorry she was. She brought with her a signed *Red* CD as well as a get well note written on a 5x7 print of herself. She told us she didn't have much stuff in her merch closet, so they stopped at Target on the way to Cedars to pick up a CD. How funny is that? I wished Lauren could have been awake to see this. Heck, I just wished Lauren was awake.

Taylor even FaceTimed with Kelsey, Ryan, and Maggie at home and was unbelievably sweet. It was nice to see them so happy if even for just a few minutes. Their world had been turned upside down and their parents weren't even with them to help them cope. Lastly, Dave and I posed for pictures with Taylor. When Bryan lifted up my phone to snap a picture for us, Taylor noticed my phone case and asked, "Is that . . . *Rick Springfield*?"

I of course proudly told her yes.

"That is so random," she said.

Obviously, *she* wasn't around in the late '80s, nothing random about my Rick. Taylor wished us well and let us know she would keep Lauren in her prayers.

Lauren's fever became more manageable throughout the day, another hurdle passed. Earlier in the week the decision was made to put Lauren into a deeper coma. She was already in a coma, but they felt they needed to put her in a drug induced coma to allow her body even more rest. She still wasn't able to get her MRI. They had had one scheduled but brought her back to her room when her heart rate dipped down to 27 beats per minute. I was in no hurry for her to have an MRI. I was doing just fine living in my fantasy world not knowing the extent of her damage.

On May 2, 2013, Lauren opened her eyes. That was what we had been waiting for. I longed to see those beautiful blue eyes.

When Lauren was a toddler, I would ask her, "What color are your eyes?"

Her response was always, "Blue and white." She was the cutest little girl in the whole world and her kind heart was unmatched. When she was little, I knew about all of her good deeds. Now that she was an adult and living on her own, I didn't witness her kindness firsthand, but since her accident I received countless emails and messages from strangers telling me stories of the many kind things that she had done for them. Why is it that we can always see those qualities in others but when they are right under our noses in our own families, we tend to take them for granted? I was proud to be her mom.

I don't know what I was expecting when she finally woke up, but it wasn't this. *This* was awful. I felt like a fraud. We had posted the great news to Caring-Bridge that Lauren had opened her eyes. All of our followers were commenting on how happy they were, and that God had answered our many prayers. Only I wasn't happy; I was miserable. She looked worse than before. When her eyes were open it was crystal clear that the lights were on, but nobody was home. I couldn't understand how someone could look so lost or unfocused.

———

With Courtney now back in LA with us, it was nice to have her positive energy fill the room every day. On May 3, I received an email from Rick Springfield's publicist (!). Someone who knew I was a fan reached out and told her about the accident. She arranged to have Rick call me the next day. I couldn't believe it. I put makeup on for the first time since I arrived in LA. That phone call did nothing to change what was going on in my life, but it gave me a huge boost in morale. To know that my teen idol cared that much to take time out of his day to offer me a few words of encouragement was mind blowing. When she beeped Rick through to the line it was amazing how calm I felt, maybe because my main focus was still on Lauren and her recovery. Rick asked about Lauren and shared how sorry he was that this happened. I don't know what came over me, but I decided to share a little story with Rick. At the time, I had a framed 5x7 picture of Dave and me on my nightstand at home next to an 8x10 picture of Rick and I from a meet and greet in 2011. I told Rick about the framed photos and that, sometimes, Dave throws a towel over the larger picture and teases, "Don't look Rick, you don't want to see what I'm about to do to her." Rick chuckled at the story and I thought to myself, *OMG, did I seriously just share that?*

We chatted for a few minutes more and I thanked him profusely for the call. Courtney recorded my end of the conversation with her cell phone and posted it on Facebook. Kelsey knew he was calling that afternoon and couldn't wait to watch the video after soccer practice. Her friends and teammates were gathered around her as the video began to play. Imagine her mortification surrounded by her friends when it got to the part about the towel. Now everyone at school knew that her parents had sex. She considered the video complete social suicide. And she wasn't the only one who felt that way—the rest of my kids reported the video as inappropriate to Facebook and it was removed.

This was our *second* social media snafu.

Our first happened while Courtney was back in NYC. *Life of the Lucys*'s blog posts were becoming very popular. People everywhere were beginning to take notice. In my eyes this newfound popularity brought more prayers for Lauren. The hospital, however, felt differently. Before Courtney got back to town, Dave and I were called back in for another conference. This conference was different; it was with people from their PR department. We sat down a little confused as to why we were there. First, they told us how sorry they were for our daughter's present condition. Next, they told us how inappropriate our social media page was to their employees and guests. I was confused until they shared some printed blog posts from *Life of the Lucys*. The first one was a photo of an older gentleman sitting on a prayer matt on the floor in the waiting room wearing a turban. The caption read: *Hurry up and wake up, Luc, this is my new roommate.*

The next little gem they slid across the table was a photo of Nurse John's butt in his hospital scrubs. The caption on that photo mentioned something about being able to bounce a quarter off of Nurse John's butt and that unfortunately Nurse John was gay (the good ones always were). Dave and I were mortified; we had no words. We apologized and let them know we would make sure the posts were removed as soon as possible. This was so much worse than the principal's office. Later in the week, Nurse John called us over to the desk and let us know *he* was not offended by Courtney's post and he actually thought it was funny. Looking back on that day I can find the humor in it. Here we were in an ICU room with a daughter who was near death and we were in a room discussing bouncing quarters off of someone's butt.

Chapter Five

MOVING TO BEVERLY HILLS

Once we realized we would be in LA for a while we knew the Marriott was not a long-term option. I needed to find an apartment close to Cedars. Lauren's employer was extremely generous and found and paid for a nice one-bedroom apartment. I felt like Elly Mae Clampett meets Arthur "The Fonze" Fonzarelli. Whether or not Beverly Hills was ready for me, here I was living behind some orthodontist's house above his three-car garage smack dab in the middle of Beverly Hills.

The day after I moved into my apartment, Dave had to fly home. It was hard for us to make the decision; our hearts were in two different places, but it was time for him to go home. He had been with me in California for two weeks. Sam had gone above and beyond. She was twenty-six, just beginning her career, and she was thrust into making lunches, driving kids to school, shuttling to soccer practices, and helping with homework. Our kids needed a parent and Sam needed her life back.

Back in LA, I would start the day with a way too strong cup of coffee made by my new roommate, Courtney. I allowed myself ten minutes to drink my coffee and pull myself together before I headed to Cedars-Sinai. One of my favorite quotes from the movie *Bridesmaids* is, "Carol! Get your sh** together, Carol." I recited that line to myself every morning. I knew I had to be strong and hold it together.

Praying with my rosary was always my first order of business. Next I would pull the chair up to Lauren's bed and try to come up with small talk. It was becoming increasingly more difficult to facilitate enough one-sided conversation to fill a twelve-hour day.

By mid-morning I would head downstairs for my Chai Tea Latte with a name on my cup that I didn't recognize. I sat in the warm sun wishing I was the other person the front of the cup said I was. This was the only part of the day when I allowed myself twenty minutes to cry. I had a favorite bench where I always sat, and if it was taken, I cried even harder. Life was hard. Many times I wondered if God was still listening and if things would ever get better.

Meanwhile, friends and family back home were doing a good job looking out for us. Meals were still being dropped off, people were fighting over who would be cutting our grass for the week, and we had enough gas, grocery and restaurant gift cards to last for months. Alex Pietrangelo from the St. Louis Blues even heard about our story and treated Dave and the kids to a Blues play-off game. David Freese and Jon Jay from the STL Cardinals tweeted out get well wishes. We felt as if the whole city of St. Louis had our backs.

When we didn't have visitors to distract us, Courtney and I had to find things to do to entertain ourselves to keep from going crazy. One of the games we would play was called "Gay or Straight." Many times we would be at lunch and after the waiter walked away one of us would ask, "Do you think he is gay or straight?" It was hard to tell. I have a friend named Joe who lives in New York. We dated briefly in high school. Joe is great but we had no chemistry. He's gay (go figure!). We kept in touch through the years and had dinner or drinks a few times when I was in New York visiting Lauren. Joe texted me one afternoon to check on Lauren's current condition and I shared with him the game that Courtney and I made up, telling him how truly hard it was to tell who was gay and who was straight in LA. After I sent the text, I hoped I didn't come across as mean. Our game wasn't malicious at all; we were just trying to pass the time. Thankfully, Joe texted right back and wrote, "That's hilarious. Check the eyebrows. If they are not plucked, they are clearly straight."

I appreciated the inside tip.

My rental apartment was a few miles away from the hospital right off of La Cienega Boulevard. Three years later Kenny Chesney and Pink came out with the song "Setting the World on Fire." It's opening lines talked about getting drunk on La Cienga Boulevard and taking photos of anyone who looked like a celebrity.

I never saw any stars, and I sure as heck never got drunk, but the song always makes me think of my little Beverly Hills apartment and our many drive-thru runs for comfort food at McDonald's. I would alternate from a Filet-o-Fish to a Quarter Pounder with Cheese, both delicious in their own right. And always with a side order of large fries! Our song would have gone: *We got fat on La Cienga Boulevard . . .*

In late May I went home for twenty-two hours to surprise Ryan and attend his eighth-grade graduation. Shannon was in LA visiting at the time; she and Courtney stayed with Lauren. I hated to leave but felt that Ryan needed me. Plus it was nice to sleep in my own bed, even for just a few hours. When I arrived home, I couldn't believe how green everything looked. When I'd left St. Louis, everything was dark and dreary. This was another sad reminder that life was moving forward without me. Lauren and I were in our own little bubble. The world inside the Saperstein Critical Care Tower was stuck in limbo while the rest of the world was still business as usual.

Life was different at home without me. Thanks to Sam's short run as the queen of the castle, Ryan and Maggie learned how to turn off a light when they left a room and to reuse a towel after taking a shower. Seamus was even back in a dog crate. Sam runs a tight ship. Ryan and Maggie were anxious for one of us to return.

Once I was back in LA, we hit another little bump.

Lauren had an area of her brain where the blood was pooling and would not drain. Dr. Chen explained he needed to operate again. The surgery was called a "wash out"—he would go in and wash out the area filled with blood. I was scared but I trusted Dr. Chen completely. Right before surgery I told him to make sure he brought his A-game. He assured me he would. After a successful surgery, we went back to the ICU; there's no need for a recovery room, as ICU patients are monitored so closely they come right back after surgery.

It was becoming increasingly difficult to stay positive. Lauren's condition remained the same. Staff would come in to move her every two hours so she wouldn't get bed sores. This was the hardest part for me to watch. All of the pinching and tubes and PICC lines and surgeries were scary, but they paled in comparison to witnessing her lifeless body as they would move her hour after hour on the count of three.

As the days passed, Lauren spent more time with her vacant eyes open. I hated seeing her like this. I remember thinking, *God forgive me, but please close your eyes, go back to sleep.*

I couldn't stand to see the blankness. This couldn't be it, could it? Could this be the way she would spend the rest of her life? I'm her mother and I was perfectly prepared to care for her in whatever capacity God gifted me, but my heart broke for how the "Old Lauren" wanted to live her life. She was a planner; she made lists and checked things off. This was not on her list!

Finally we were able to get her MRI results, which didn't tell us anything good. Dr Yen came in after seeing the results and walked in with his head hung low. By then Dr. Yen had learned to love us and became almost warm or fuzzy, but definitely not warm *and* fuzzy. Baby steps. He shared that there was damage throughout Lauren's brain. The bulk of the damage was located on her left side— the side that took the brunt of the impact. It was explained to me that she flew through the air with such velocity that the damage was throughout her brain, mimicking that of a child who suffered shaken baby syndrome. He described her injuries as "catastrophic." Not exactly the best news I heard all day. When he finished, he looked at me and in his thick accent said, "She young. We wait and see."

Lauren has always had the ability to win people over. I was impressed that even in a semi vegetative state she still had the mojo to make a doctor completely alter his bedside manner.

Although up to then things had remained uncertain and Lauren's future was unknown, I had an overwhelming sense of peace that things would be okay. I attributed that to my strong faith. After hearing her results, my faith was still strong, but it was wavering fast. I was back to pleading with God, hoping that the doctors were all wrong. Dr. Chen arrived later in the day. He sat down next to me to further talk about the results. There was no denying the amount of brain damage we were dealing with. He looked at me with compassion and his words went something like, "If you were to ask me if she would ever be able to live on her own independently in New York again, I would have to say I don't know. What I *can* tell you with certainty is that it is not out of the realm of possibilities."

That was all I needed to hear; my faith had been restored. Obviously, there were no guarantees, but Dr. Chen gave me hope. Weeks earlier we had heard from Dr. Yen that Lauren would never be the same, ever again. He told us she may always be in a wheelchair and we might need to look at long-term care facilities as a real possibility because her injuries were so severe.

Those seven words from Dr. Chen became my new mantra: *Not out of the realm of possibilities.*

That along with our existing family mantra: *Murphys Don't Quit!*

"Murphys Don't Quit" was something that Dave always said to the kids when they were little—no matter the situation. If they wanted to quit going to dance class or quit a softball team or even a task like pairing up socks . . . Murphys Don't Quit! Pairing socks was always my go-to punishment when the kids were in trouble. With a household of nine, many times it was easier to buy new socks instead of finding a pair that actually matched. The second the kids would start to complain and want to quit, Dave would remind them, "Murphys Don't Quit!

Shannon designed *Murphys Don't Quit* support t-shirts. We also sold thousands of *Murphys Don't Quit* bracelets—both items in powder blue, Lauren's favorite color. We never knew the magnitude those words would take on. Lauren became the true embodiment of the phrase, *Murphys Don't Quit!*

At the time of her accident, Lauren had a boyfriend. They were only around four months into their relationship. I had met him a couple of times—once in New York when Dave and I visited in March of that year, and again in St. Louis when he came to my nephew's wedding two weeks before the accident. From what I knew of him, he was a great guy. He flew to LA a few weeks after the accident. Lauren was still in a semi vegetative state and seemed unaware of everyone and everything. I know it had to be really tough on him. She looked terrible. Her head was sunken in where her skull was missing, so she looked like an alien. Her hair had grown back a bit and he laughed when he said, "She's a redhead. Who knew?"

While he was there, I noticed all the little things about him: how he waited for all of the women to exit the elevator before he did, how he thanked all of the nurses for taking such good care of Lauren, how he chewed so quietly (unlike my husband), how comfortable he seemed to just sit and hold Lauren's hand, and how incredibly sad his eyes looked. I sat across from him at lunch one afternoon looking at him, like *really* looking at him. He was blond and had beautiful bright blue eyes. I imagined how striking their children could have been and silently I grieved for a dream that I knew would never come to be.

Kelsey had to schedule her visit around her soccer schedule. She came for a few days just before the team had their district play-off tournament. When she came into Lauren's room for the first time she got really emotional. Dr. Chen was present when she walked in, and seeing her reaction really got to him. He walked over to Kelsey, asked her if she had any questions, and let her know it was okay to be upset. Seeing her big sister like that was really tough. I was so touched at how kind and sensitive Dr. Chen was that my mind wondered for a second if maybe Dr. Chen was gay? Then I looked at his eyebrows—clearly Dr. Chen has never used a tweezer in his life. I almost giggled as I stood there watching my seventeen-year-old daughter being comforted by her sister's brain surgeon. *Dear God, I have officially lost my ever-living mind!*

Kelsey made music CDs for the staff at Cedars-Sinai. She labeled the one for Dr. Chen "Derek Shepherd AKA McDreamy." The cute neuro doc with the sexy South African accent got one labeled "McSteamy." It was so cute watching Kelsey walk the halls of the ICU handing out her gift CDs to all the doctors and nurses and thanking everyone for taking such good care of her big sister.

All of my kids had a chance to visit, except my two youngest. The little ones did not want to come. Ryan asked if it would be okay if he waited for Lauren's hair to grow back. I let him know that of course it was. There was no right answer, no parenting manual on how to get through this. I knew they all loved their sister and there was no blueprint in regard to if and when they came to visit.

Shannon was in town the day Lauren finally made it out of the ICU. After five long weeks, it was time to transition to a regular floor. Going to the regular floor was scary. Shannon and I made the decision to spend the night with her. We weren't comfortable leaving her overnight, especially after meeting her new nurse.

Lauren's new nurse was named Nic—not Nick but Nic, Nick without a *k*. Nic let Shannon and I know how great of a nurse he was and that his first order of business was to go over Lauren with a fine-tooth comb to make sure she didn't have any skin breakdowns or other issues that could have occurred during her time in ICU.

It felt as if Nic wasn't concerned that Lauren had some health issues he wanted to address; he just wanted to make sure that no one would accuse him of those types of things happening on his watch. Nic called his aide Katie in to assist him as he went over every inch of Lauren's broken body like an Enterprise Rent-A-Car employee pointing out the scratches, dents, and dings before the customer rolls off the lot. Nic rolled her body from side to side as I painfully watched him examine her as if she wasn't even human. I wanted to scream. I missed the comfort of the ICU; this was not what I was expecting. I hated our new room and I hated Nic.

KEY 1: SHOW UP

The first key is simple, show up! All of us have days where we'd rather stay in bed with the covers over our heads. In all honesty, since Lauren's accident, I have had several days where that is exactly what I've done. Did those days make me feel any better? The answer is a resounding *no*. Bad things don't go away just because you refuse to show up.

Many people showed up on April 19, 2013. The first responders, the witnesses, the detective, the hospital social worker, the ER staff, Dr. Chen, Nurse Becky, Nurse John . . . the list is endless. I think it's safe to assume that all of them woke up that morning expecting a typical workday (like I did). Imagine if Dr. Chen would have called in sick?

A few days after the accident, Lance Bass, Joey Fatone, Taylor Swift, and Rick Springfield made the decision to show up, too. Like seriously, Rick Springfield called me—OMG! These famous people did not know us, but people who did made the gracious decision to show up, reach out to them, and find a way to lift our spirits.

Before Lauren's accident I would hear stories about tragic events, pause a minute, say a quick prayer, and move on. If they weren't someone in my inner circle, I wouldn't even consider reaching out. That would be weird, right? Now I realize how much my own insecurities blocked me from showing up to help others.

The voicemail messages, emails, texts, and Facebook posts from friends, family, and friends of friends became my kryptonite. I was so honored and humbled by people I vaguely knew—or in many cases, didn't know at all. These acts of kindness were what made me feel as if the whole universe was on my side.

One day, a rental car just showed up at the hospital. Someone named Mike who I went to church with in our previous neighborhood decided to show up in a big way. Mike wasn't in my inner circle, yet he decided to show up and help without being asked. He took care of the bill for the length of my stay in Los Angeles (forty-seven days). Wow!

It is truly a gift that we all have the power to show up and brighten someone else's day.

I wish I could have a do-over for all the times I failed to show up for people. I will never let my own insecurities get in the way of helping others.

Let's face it, life is messy; each one of us knows someone who, right now, at this very moment, is going through something tough. It doesn't have to be a tragic event; it could be a job loss, an illness, a break-up, or basically anything that is causing pain.

Don't think about. Put your ego to the side and show up!

Chapter Six

HELLO CHICAGO

Lauren was finally considered stable. My fear of her dying had morphed into a new fear of her just *existing* without any real quality of life. Her eyes remained blank and unfocused; they were able to do what the doctor's called *track*. Tracking is a big step after brain injury. Doctors would hold an 8x10 photo of our family inches away from Lauren's face and then slowly move it up or down or right or left, hoping her eyes would follow the movement. Occasionally her eyes would move in the right direction. This was considered a *win*. Although, I felt her eye movement was more of a coincidence, I was happy that the doctors felt differently and that she was finally doing something right in a neuro test.

To be honest, I wasn't quite sure what they were seeing. To me, it looked like her eyes were still lost within her soul and she had no clue the picture was even in the room, much less inches from her face.

Every morning doctors would come in and say, "Good morning, Lauren. Can you give me a thumbs up?"

Lauren would always look at them blankly.

"How about two fingers? Can you show me two fingers?"

The response was always the same, *nothing*. I knew that these tests were necessary, but I secretly wished they would just stop asking.

Nurses would put Lauren in a cardiac chair every day for a few hours. This was apparently good for her; I had my doubts. When they did this, she had to wear a helmet to protect her head because her bone flap was still missing. She started this a few days before we left ICU. Erin was in town the day they initially brought us the helmet—another reminder of how broken Lauren was. We decided if she had to wear this bulky, ugly helmet, we were going to do our best to spruce it up. We ran over to Target and bought craft supplies. The next time Lauren was in the cardiac chair she was sporting a helmet with a pink sparkly 3D crown glued on top, as well as her name in great big blue sparkly letters across the front.

We had officially lost our minds. Lauren looked ridiculous.

Now that we were on the regular floor, the cardiac chair made me more nervous. To put her in, they would lay the chair flat, slide it next to her bed, and with the help of staff slide her over to the chair on the count of three, using her draw sheet (basically a top sheet they lay under the patient to assist with moving them to another position). Once there, they folded the chair back to a chair position and went on their way.

It would never take long before Lauren was sliding down the chair. She was sitting on a slippery sheet that was on top of a slippery vinyl chair. She had no muscle control; gravity always took over.

The first few times I would call for help. (They always took forever to show up.) Eventually I learned to figure it out myself. I would keep a supply of pillows, towels, washcloths, or basically anything I could get my hands on to help prop up her slumping body to keep her from falling out of the chair. There was a safety strap across the waist to keep her in, yet I wasn't overly confident of that strap. Lauren was under 100 lbs. and I was pretty confident if I wasn't there, she would be sliding right under it like queen of the limbo game. Her head was the worst. Her helmet/tiara was top heavy and *always* fell to one side.

I hated when she was in this chair because I spent the whole time realizing how ill-equipped I was to care for her.

I hoped and prayed that Lauren knew who I was; I had no way of knowing what her brain was able to process. She was nonverbal and showed very little facial expression. One afternoon when Shannon was with me, we had the TV on watching *Keeping Up with the Kardashians*. The TV showed a close shot of Kris Jenner when Lauren lifted her head off the pillow for the first time. She leaned forward and lifted her index finger in the air as if she had an idea. I had been waiting for a moment like this, a moment when Lauren would recognize someone. I always assumed it would be me or Dave or one of the kids. I never imagined it would be Kris Jenner. Shannon and I were dying laughing. We knew this was a milestone. We took it as a win and realized that this was also typical Lauren—she was in complete control.

Soon after being transferred to the floor, Lauren had had her third brain surgery. Lauren's lumbar drain was no longer working and Dr. Chen thought it would be best to replace her bone flap sooner rather than later. A prosthetic skull had been custom-made based on her scans. Having her bone flap replaced so soon was not the norm; most TBI patients have it replaced much later. Lauren proved yet again that she was less than typical.

Dr. Chen had been waiting for the arrival of her skull before he scheduled her surgery. Lauren's increasingly worse daily neuro checks caused them to rush the order. We were literally waiting on the FedEx man to deliver my daughter's new skull. When it finally arrived, Dr. Chen brought it to show me. I don't know what I was expecting, but it wasn't what he revealed. My only knowledge of prosthetic skulls had been from the movie *National Lampoon's Christmas Vacation*. In the scene just before Clark and Cousin Eddie take off down the snow-covered hill, Eddie mentions he has a plate in his head. My hope was that hers would be different than Eddie's—he peed his pants and forget who he was every time someone used a microwave. Lucky for Lauren, the prosthetic skull was plastic. The prosthesis reminded me of a cross between an athletic cup and a hockey mask. It was hard plastic and had holes throughout the entire piece.

Several years prior, I had a bad experience with an athletic cup. Ryan was four and had just started playing ice hockey. Dave worked nights at the time, so I was in charge of getting Ryan ready for his first hockey practice. I explained to Ryan why he had to wear a cup and put it on for him. Based on the male anatomy the triangle-shaped athletic cup obviously goes with the pointy side facing upward. Ryan did not have a good experience on the ice and his little legs were a little scratched up from his mother's inability to be a competent boy mom. I was then banned from helping my son with anything penis-related.

The time was approaching for Lauren to move to an inpatient rehabilitation facility. Cedars-Sinai had done all that they could do. Lauren began breathing on her own before she was transferred out of the ICU. She was still receiving oxygen through her trach, but no longer needed the ventilator. This was a huge step and a big factor in finding the right rehab hospital. Most will not accept patients that are still vent dependent. Lauren was covered under workman's comp insurance because she had been on a business trip at the time of the accident. We didn't know it at the time but having work comp would be one of our greatest blessings. Because it was in their best interest for Lauren to recover, they were very generous with her medical needs. Dave had been in contact with her assigned insurance adjuster, who mentioned moving Lauren to a rehab facility in Chicago called RIC, The Rehab Institute of Chicago. I wanted to bring her home to St. Louis; I missed my family. We lived in a big city. I was confident we had something just as good for Lauren there. One of the Neuro ICU doctors was originally from St. Louis and thankfully I mentioned to her that Lauren's insurance company suggested RIC.

I was surprised by her response. "If you are able to be accepted to RIC, go and don't look back."

I was so naïve; I figured all rehab hospitals were pretty much the same. I didn't realize it then but RIC would become one of the greatest decisions that we made.

Once we received word that RIC agreed to take her, Cedars-Sinai's social workers worked to set up Lauren's transport to Chicago. We were planning to go by air ambulance. I was more than ready to leave LA but a little scared to go in an air ambulance. Dave flew to LA a few days before our discharge to help with the move. I had accumulated a lot of stuff, mainly due to the countless care packages people had sent. I was only allowed to bring one small suitcase with me on the plane.

Dr. Chen came by Lauren's room the night before we left to say goodbye. The ambulance was scheduled to be at the hospital around 5:30 a.m., Wednesday, June 5. We thanked Dr. Chen for all that he had done for us. He then shared that when Lauren came in to the ER, he had to make the decision on whether or not to operate. Had she been older or not in such good physical shape, he may not have made the same decision. Many factors are considered—most importantly, what would her quality of life look like if she survived. Without that surgery, she wouldn't still be with us. Dr. Chen looked at us with tears in his eyes and said, "I am so thankful that I made the right call!"

"We are, too, Dr. Chen."

He gave us hugs and then handed us his business card. He rarely gave out his personal information, but Lauren was special, and he wanted to stay in touch. We were very sad to see Dr. Jay Chen walk away. I felt like we owed so much to him. His talented hands saved my daughter's life. He would always hold a special place deep within my heart.

———

We arrived at the hospital bright and early Wednesday morning, ready for the next adventure. Lauren's flight team of nurses came to transport her to the private airport. We were surprised to see that Dr. Chen made it by in time for one last goodbye as Lauren was being wheeled down the hall. We took the elevators to the main floor and cut through the emergency room toward the ambulance entrance. I felt a large lump in my throat as we crossed over the threshold of the double doors leading toward the waiting ambulance, my mind wandering back to forty-seven days earlier when Lauren had been wheeled across that very threshold, a face without a name. I felt like jumping through that door and screaming, "Heck yeah, Trauma Foxtrot 5395 has left the building!"

Dave and I said our goodbyes and off Lauren and I went towards Bob Hope Airport in Burbank.

The private jet we boarded was super tiny. It was barely big enough for Lauren's gurney and two nurses—not exactly how I envisioned my first time in a private jet. I think it's safe to say, Beverly Hills and private jets were not near as glamorous as I had envisioned. Before take-off, the life flight nurses had to go through the safety features and crash-landing instructions the same way they do on a commercial flight. This was different. I had to pay attention because I was the only passenger on the plane who was capable of paying attention. Seated in the back of the plane, I was able to see everything that was going on, including the pilot and co-pilot. Lauren's gurney was positioned against the wall on the right side of the cabin, one nurse seated across from her and another at her feet.

Lauren was covered with a hot pink fuzzy blanket, a gift from a friend. She was wearing her Prafo boots, which were big bulky black medical boots to help prevent her from experiencing a nerve condition called drop foot. The day she received her boots, Courtney taped red construction paper to the bottom of them and wrote "Louboutin" across the middle to mimic those crazy expensive red-bottomed high heel shoes. Lauren had been in these boots for so long, the construction paper had faded and was tattered around the edges.

The airplane seats were a dirty beige-colored leather. I couldn't help but notice how old and worn the seats were, especially around the perimeter of the seat. The walls reminded me of my old conversion van, the same type of ugly patterned fabric. My old van was a 1995 GMC. *Dear God, how* old *is this plane?*

I remembered the day we bought the van. We had five kids and Lauren was nine at the time. Dave and I were twenty-seven years old, trying to raise five little girls the best we could. We were a one-car family. Money was tight. My mother-in-law won a car in our church raffle and generously gave us her old car. We traded in our existing car and picked the cheapest van on the lot, a leftover model from the previous year. That van was a godsend for us; we were finally able to fit our entire family in one vehicle and I was no longer chained to the house all day. I prayed this plane was not the last one on the lot in 1996, especially since it was 2013. Thankfully we had an uneventful flight, other than me having to pee. The nurses told me at take-off that if I needed to go to the bathroom during our flight I could pee in a cup and they have a solution that could turn the liquid to solid. I wondered if anyone ever actually peed in a cup in front of nurses and pilots on an air ambulance.

An ambulance was waiting for us when we landed in Chicago. Thirty minutes later, we were in the lobby of RIC. I waited at the front desk for a badge while they took Lauren upstairs to be admitted. There weren't any empty rooms on the brain injury floor, so she was being admitted to the stroke floor until space became available.

I walked down the hall to her temporary room with nervous anticipation. I was counting on her time here at RIC to be life-altering. I was banking on a full recovery. Lauren was assigned to the bed closest to the door. Her roommate was an older woman recovering from a stroke. Lauren looked out of place in this setting.

Dr. Ballard, the head honcho of the TBI floor came down to meet Lauren. My first impression of Dr. Ballard was that he had a warm, inviting personality, and was extremely down to earth. He appeared to be young despite his completely bald head. He had a face full of faded freckles and because of his reddish eyebrows I could tell that when he had hair, it was red. Since I have raised a few redheads myself, this told me that I needed to be prepared for bouts of stubbornness.

Dr. Ballard was impressed with Lauren's condition; he had been going over her medical records and expected her to be in much worse shape. I was delighted to hear that he was impressed with how well he felt she was doing, but I was still a little confused as to how he thought she looked good. She had the worst haircut in the history of haircuts. Back at Cedars, once they began giving Lauren regular sponge baths, the rat's nest on the top of her head had to be addressed. I reluctantly agreed to let them shave it off. Now her hair was either completely shaved or different lengths on every remaining section. She had just undergone her third brain surgery. I think Dr. Chen was afraid of my reaction if he shaved Lauren's whole head. Instead, he shaved a three-inch-wide section starting above her left eyebrow on the top of her head, ending in a large sideways "U" outlining the whole left side. In between those shaved sections were dozens and dozens of blood-stained staples, as well as a few stitches holding her scalp together. The staples wrapped around to the front of her face eventually ending on the side of her lower cheek next to her earlobe. Not a good look!

After surgery, Lauren's forehead had a large indentation where the prosthetic piece failed to create a symmetrical look. I knew how important Lauren's appearance was to her, so her forehead made me sad to look at. I wasn't prepared for her head to be so misshaped. The stitches and staples along with her haircut were temporary; the dip in her forehead was devastatingly unexpected and permanent.

Dr. Ballard mentioned that he was very pleased with the care she had received while at Cedars-Sinai. In most cases, he spends much of the first few days of a patient's care reversing their previous medication lists and treatment plans. I was happy, we were ahead of the game already. Dr. Ballard was the type of guy to roll up his sleeves and get right to work. I knew we were in the right place.

Lauren still had a PICC line in place in her upper arm. Dr. Ballard explained it was no longer needed and planned on having it removed later in the week. He also told us it was time to say goodbye to the trach. I was happy at the prospect of getting rid of the trach but also a little confused. Lauren's trach required frequent suctioning; lung congestion is a common issue for patient's that are unable to move about on their own. I was unsure as to how Lauren would be able to clear the mucus in her lungs if her trach waere removed. I didn't question his recommendations but was sure as heck going to check with Google as soon as he left the room.

Dave arrived in Chicago a few hours later. Sitting in Lauren's room was hard; we didn't have much privacy or space. There would be no therapy today, yet tomorrow we were to hit the ground running. The minutes on the clock felt more like hours. Dave went to get the keys to my new apartment; I wasn't ready to leave Lauren alone in a new place just yet. I waited with her while Dave took care of moving my stuff and getting to know the lay of the land.

My new Chicago apartment was a little less than a mile away from RIC. Sam had put something on Lauren's CaringBridge site that we were looking for housing in Chicago. Many people came forward offering support. One offer was too good to be true—the president of Loyola University Chicago was the brother to Sam's boyfriend's longtime family friend. How is that for a connection? He graciously offered a Loyola apartment free of charge. This apartment came with a washer and dryer and was fully furnished. It was such a blessing. Lauren has an uncanny gift of finding the most expensive cites in the country to live in: New York, LA, and now Chicago. She obviously thought she was born with a silver spoon in her mouth, instead of the reality of mismatched, bendable dollar store spoons.

A nurse printed Lauren's schedule for the next day. Schedules come out every day, late afternoon. Each patient keeps their schedule taped to a closet door. Inside the closet held Lauren's personal belongings, as well as all of her new supplies. These included a pack of adult diapers and wet wipes. Lauren still had a catheter while at Cedars and the absorbent disposable pad on her bed always took care of bowel movements. Simply hearing the word "diapers" was like a knife in my heart. I'm not sure why it bothered me so much. Was it *really* that different from having a catheter in place for months and pooping in your bed? Somehow it felt different. I hated it and I knew how mortified Lauren would be if she knew this was happening.

I was anxious to check out my new apartment but waited until later in the evening when Lauren was ready for bed before leaving for the night. Saying I was waiting for her to be ready for bed sounds funny because Lauren was always *in* bed. But in my head, it made it easier to leave if I told myself that she was ready for bed. The reality of the situation was that I left every evening when I had had enough. I could only spend so many hours sitting in an uncomfortable chair, hoping and praying that the daughter, whom I had spent twenty-five years loving and nurturing, was still somewhere within this broken, emaciated body before me.

Back in my apartment I felt grateful that I had a place to stay within walking distance to Lauren and within driving distance to the rest of my family. For now, I was content, and it felt good to be able to sleep again in the loving, strong arms of my husband.

Chapter Seven

MOVING RIGHT ALONG

I was impressed with RIC. Each floor even had a gym at the end of the hall. Lauren hadn't been fitted for a wheelchair yet, so the therapist showed up with a sling apparatus that scooped Lauren up, hooked to a crane type thing, and wheeled her down to the gym. I liked how her therapist, a petite girl, seemed to take charge and not be afraid of Lauren's fragile little body (which was more than I could say for myself). I hoped I wouldn't always feel so inadequate. In the gym, Lauren was put in a seated position on the mat and her therapist sat behind her. I suddenly understand why her lungs would no longer be full of mucous; RIC had no intention of letting Lauren remain inactive.

Before Lauren's session finished, we received word that a room had opened up on the TBI floor. Once we got settled into Lauren's new room, I knew we had to find a way to make it look less like a hospital. I called Erin and let her know that our first order of business would be decorating Lauren's room. We had all felt helpless for so long; I think Erin was happy to finally have something she could do for Lauren.

Erin asked about a budget. I laughed and said, "No budget."

Dave was sitting near me and rolled his eyes. He has learned through the years not to complain, otherwise I spend double.

Most of our kids were coming up for the weekend. The apartment wasn't big enough for all of us, so RIC generously offered a couple of rooms at the nearby Ronald McDonald House.

Lauren now had her own wheelchair. Because Lauren was so small, her wheelchair parts were made for a child. The frame was hot pink, and the leg rests were neon green. When Lauren was in her wheelchair, her head would fall forward and gravity made it hard for her to control her saliva. She was learning to swallow in speech therapy and her therapist Jim was working on head control. Again, I hated seeing her like this. She looked much better when she was in bed. Unfortunately this wasn't about when she looks better, it was about the best way for her to *get better,* regardless of whether or not it made her mother sad to watch her sit in a wheelchair and drool.

Grandma and the kids arrived right before Lauren's physical therapy session. Lauren's therapist Jim was receptive to a few of her siblings tagging along to watch. He was already used to me coming along to every therapy session, what's a few more? For whatever reason, Jim decided to move Lauren to a standing position to see how she would react. She looked like a hot mess. Her right arm was continuing to get worse and was all curled up like a pretzel against her chest. Her head was hanging down and she was wearing hot pink glow-in-the-dark skeleton pajamas. When Jim lifted her from the mat to a standing position, despite her inability to comprehend what was going on, she took a step. He looked surprised and said, "I didn't expect *that* to happen."

I felt as if that one step was the equivalent of her winning the decathlon. It was what I believed would be the first of many triumphs for Miss Lauren Murphy. I knew that she had only just begun. While we were at Lauren's therapy session, Erin decorated Lauren's room. In true Murphy form, the room looked a bit obnoxious. Erin covered every inch of it that was allowed. The rules stated that we couldn't put tape on the walls, but nothing stated "No tape on the ugly artwork."

Finally, Lauren's room felt less like a hospital and more like home.

Later that evening we left RIC and went to an Italian restaurant near the Ronald McDonald House. There were eight of us: Dave and I, my mom, Erin, Shannon, Kelsey, Ryan, and Maggie. Typically, when I left Lauren, I grabbed something quick to eat on my walk home and went to bed. Tonight was different. We were having a family sit-down dinner. It felt almost normal. After dinner, the kids sat around the table telling family stories, talking, and laughing. This was the first time our family had been together in months. I knew how much they had all missed having both of their parents in the same room. It was well overdue. Grandma was always willing to pitch in and be a stand in for us but it wasn't the same, they needed both of their parents. The longer we sat in that restaurant, the more I was consumed with guilt. I felt like the worst mother in the history of the world. Here I was, laughing and talking, while one of my daughters was a few blocks away, all alone in a hospital. I couldn't shake the stark contrast of each scenario.

Back at the apartment, I shared with Dave how much I hated being at dinner. I didn't feel like it was fair to Lauren if I was out having fun. Dave helped me understand how important it was for our other kids to be able to still enjoy my company. I knew he was right, but I still felt lousy. Laughter was always a big part of everything that I did. One of the greatest gifts I inherited from my late father is my ability to find humor in everything, even the hard stuff. This was different. I no longer wanted to laugh. I didn't feel like being funny.

By Monday of the next week, Lauren's PICC line and trach were removed. She walked on a treadmill wearing a harness and was learning to swallow small teaspoons of water. I was amazed at how quickly she was advancing. Her right arm was still spastic but her right leg was beginning to move a little with the help of Jim.

With my family back in St. Louis, I was ready to dive in headfirst. Lauren's therapists were busy teaching me how to help care for Lauren. There was a task sheet on the front of Lauren's closet and her therapists would check off each task as I mastered them. I was eager to get as many check marks as I could. We started with things like helping Lauren dress and changing her diapers. These tasks were difficult because Lauren was still unable to help by moving her body. Who knew there was an actual technique? As the mother of seven, I have changed more than my fair share of diapers, yet this was entirely different.

I wanted to learn; I was tired of waiting on staff to come to the rescue every time she had a bowel movement. When they took too long, I was always dangerously close to running into the hallway and having a Shirley MacLaine moment like in the movie *Terms of Endearment* when her character screamed at the nurses who took too long to bring her daughter's pain medication. I felt it was up to me to make sure Lauren got what she needed, and I hated being dependent on other people to care for her. Back when my kids were little, I was never nearly as quick to change a diaper as I was now, especially if I noticed they were wet or dirty during *Days of Our Lives*. I raised my babies back in the pioneer days. I never had a pause button on my TV and programming a VCR seemed as if it required a college degree or a Mensa membership card.

My diaper changing days spanned over a fourteen-year period. I enjoyed a nice break from 1989 to 1991, as Lauren was potty trained before her second birthday. I remember thinking she must have been gifted. How many kids are completely potty-trained before their second birthday? Imagine my surprise when she enrolled in preschool and I found out that she wasn't gifted. Instead, she was just like all the other preschoolers, if by far the cutest kid in the class but maybe not Harvard bound. Erin was born when Lauren was four, ending my two-year break from diapers. The rest of the Murphy kids were spaced an average of two years apart. For the next twelve years, diapers were an everyday part of my life. Obviously, Dave and I were failing miserably at the dangerous game of "Vatican Roulette."

At RIC, Lauren began throwing up several times a day. The first time it happened was in the elevator as we were transferring from the stroke floor to the brain injury unit. This continued for a couple of weeks. Dr. Ballard was growing concerned with her many bouts of nausea and ordered a CT scan. Northwestern Memorial Hospital was only a few blocks away, so Lauren went by wheelchair.

Her nurse that day got her checked in, then looked at me and said, "I think she's in good hands. The hospital will call me when she is finished."

I was confused; this was Lauren's second trip to Northwestern for a CT scan. The first time she was brought very early, before I arrived, and a nurse accompanied her the whole time. I was a little nervous but didn't say anything, as I was afraid to come across as someone who was afraid to be alone with their own daughter. *What could go wrong?* I thought.

Famous last words.

The first issue we had was that they needed a urine sample before they could do the CT scan to confirm she wasn't pregnant. She no longer had a catheter; a urine sample wouldn't be as simple without a catheter. I explained to the nurses that Lauren had a pregnancy test at Cedars-Sinai upon admission, as well as at

Northwestern two weeks earlier (when she still had her catheter), and both tests confirmed she was not pregnant. She had been either in a coma or a vegetative state since April. Lauren's endometriosis and her inability to live with spider veins, caused her OBGYN to substitute the medication that put her in a false state of menopause with an IUD which not only prevented agonizing endometriosis pain, it also prevented pregnancy.

I was pretty positive that my brain-injured daughter was not also dealing with unplanned pregnancy. They wouldn't budge, this was hospital protocol. So, we waited, and waited, and waited. Finally, at least an hour later a nurse came in with a catheter and emptied Lauren's bladder to do the pregnancy test. Surprise surprise, she was cleared to go to radiology.

Lauren came back after her CT scan and we waited again for the all clear from the radiologist. While we were waiting Lauren had a bowel movement. Lauren's diaper leaked through her pants and was all over the bed. I called the nurse button for help, and they brought me supplies and a pair of clean scrub pants. I muddled through as best as I could; I had just been trained the previous week.

Once I had her cleaned up, I had to call for help to move her to the wheelchair, so they could change the sheet. Once finished, the nurse helped me move Lauren back to the bed. Her bed was an older style, the kind with the thick metal rails and no buttons to easily adjust the bed up or down. As soon as the nurse left the room, Lauren began to throw up. While at RIC I had learned how important it was to keep her head up when she vomited, otherwise it posed a danger of her aspirating, Lauren was still receiving all nourishment through her feeding tube. Her feedings were similar to baby formula in look as well as smell. When Lauren threw up at RIC it reminded me of when she was an infant and would projectile vomit. Now as Lauren began to throw up, I rushed to her bedside to try and pull her head up. The big bulky bars were preventing me from reaching her.

Her call button was on the other side of her, out of my reach. I was on my tippy toes—I'm only 5'1"—and the high bars prevented me from reaching her head. I couldn't find the latch to lower the bar, all I could do was hoist my body across the bar and, in this position, get her head a few inches off the pillow. My arms were not long enough, or strong enough, to lift her shoulders. I awkwardly held her head up as she continued to vomit all over both of us.

As I teetered across the bar, balancing myself with my ribcage, I was finally able to reach the call button. I held back the flood of tears as help finally arrived. The nurse lowered the bar and propped up bed while Lauren continued to get sick. Once she finished, they brought me wet washcloths to clean her up, more clean scrubs, and a new hospital gown. I put Lauren in dry clothes and blotted my shirt dry as best as I could. I was soaked through my bra with vomit. Despite my normal optimism, I felt helpless and inadequate.

Caring for Lauren was tough. I was afraid I would never feel capable. Eventually a doctor came in to explain why we had the longer than usual wait. Lauren's brain ventricles showed on her scans to be enlarged. The radiologist was afraid Lauren needed immediate surgery. He ordered a consult with her new neurosurgeon, Dr. Langdon, as well as Dr. Ballard. Both doctors agreed that Lauren needed surgery to install a ventricular shunt, but they didn't feel it needed to be done immediately. The plan was to schedule her surgery later in the week. I had no idea that while I was up to my elbows in diarrhea and vomit, discussions were going on amongst Lauren's doctors involving a much needed fourth brain surgery. I was sitting impatiently in the corner of the room feeling miserable when the doctor came in to talk to me. I had a bag full of foul-smelling wet clothes at my feet, my chest area was soaking wet, I was freezing cold, and I smelled like rotten baby formula. Hearing that she needed more brain surgery was unexpected. Suddenly my cold wet shirt and bag of diarrhea smelling clothes seemed rather insignificant.

Back at RIC, I didn't even mention to anyone the issues I had while at the hospital. I decided I would just make sure I was better prepared next time and would speak up if I felt uncomfortable. Dr. Langdon came to talk to me later that afternoon about Lauren's shunt surgery. I really liked him—he was friendly and warm, just like Dr. Chen. We were lucky to have found two brain surgeons who had personalities. Dr. Langdon attended medical school in St. Louis and was originally from New York. I knew Lauren would have loved that he was a New Yorker and *I* loved that he had lived in St. Louis.

When Dr. Langdon talked to me, he also talked to Lauren. I liked that about him, even though Lauren made no facial expressions or showed any sign that she knew someone was speaking. He treated her like she mattered, like a real person, not someone who used to be a real person. I felt ashamed because I often struggled with that myself and I am her mother. I hated that she needed another surgery. Her body had already been through enough but Dr. Langdon made me feel more at ease.

The morning of Lauren's surgery, I dressed her in a *Don't Worry I Got This* t-shirt. A nurse attached a dozen sponge-like round stickers all over Lauren's forehead, then drew big circles around each sticker with a purple marker. I believe they planned to attach some sort of electrode to those stickers later. After she finished covering Lauren in weird looking foam stickers, she sent us back to the waiting room. As I sat in this large room, I realized we must have been quite a sight: the bad haircut, the mismatched clown-colored wheelchair, the stickers and purple markings all over her forehead. Suddenly, it dawned on me that maybe the *Don't Worry I Got This* t-shirt wasn't the best choice for today.

We headed down to pre-op, where I was happy to help her change out of the t-shirt into a hospital gown. The nurse who was doing her pre-op questions was someone I will never forget. He was middle-aged, medium build as well as height, and wore blue scrub pants that tied at the waist. I couldn't help but notice how extremely fit he was despite being well over forty. I felt his warmth and kindness the minute he walked in; his eyes were kind and his eyebrows were perfectly plucked. Many of the questions he asked were the typical surgery questions:

"When was the last time she ate or drank? Ever had a bad reaction to anesthesia? What is her surgical history? Etc."

With each question I had to go down the list of accident-related surgical procedures; although the list was a mile long, those weren't the tough ones to talk about. The tough ones were listing the childhood surgeries. *The tubes in her ears as an infant, the tonsillectomy she had at age four.* Thinking back to those surgeries made me feel nostalgic. After Lauren's tonsillectomy, her surgeon gave us a jar of formaldehyde containing her enlarged tonsils. I remember laughing when he handed them to Dave and said, "Here Dad, you paid for them." Lauren loved showing off her tonsils to anyone and everyone who came to our house. We eventually talked her into letting us throw her disintegrating tonsils under the kitchen sink in the trash.

Sitting in that room listing her prior surgeries made me think back as to how frightened I had been to watch my sweet little girl with her mountain of messy strawberry blond curls being wheeled off to surgery. Listing her past surgeries, including her two fairly recent endometriosis surgeries, felt trivial in comparison to present-day Lauren.

When we finished all the required medical questions, he looked at me with tenderness and said, "Your daughter is so lucky to have a mom like you. Can I give you a hug?"

I needed that hug. It was my best hug ever. I will never forget that hug, nor will I ever forget him or his kindness.

They were ready for Lauren; it was time for me to say my goodbye. Her nurse said to her, "Tell your mom goodbye."

My lip quivered as I held back my tears and kissed her cheek. I was heart-broken, not because she was headed back for brain surgery but because she was incapable of telling me goodbye. Did she even know who I was? I hoped so but I had no way of knowing. She couldn't talk or even show facial expressions. She was moments away from her fourth brain surgery. She wasn't scared or anxious; she was void of all expression. It was so depressing. I left the pre-op area and took the elevator to the surgery waiting room. Finding a spot in the corner away from most of the other people, I wished Dave could have been with me, but he had used all of his time off from work. I had been through this before at Cedars and knew I would be okay. But I wasn't okay; I was scared, and I was all alone.

As I sat in that room I couldn't stop the flood of tears. My mind raced back to Lauren's childhood and to all of the mistakes that I had made. I kept thinking, *Why didn't I read to her more?* All kids loved to be read to, I never made the time. Many nights I didn't even tuck her in, I just gave her a goodnight kiss from the living room or kitchen, or wherever I happened to be at bedtime. *Why didn't I stop and appreciate the little things?* I was always exhausted and so anxious for my day to end. I should have spent more nights giving back scratches or having impromptu dance parties in the kitchen.

I wondered if she knew how much I loved her. I felt like I had failed as a mother and she deserved so much more than what I gave her. I was always so busy with the younger kids; I could have done so much better; I should have done so much better.

Dr. Langdon came to find me when he finished Lauren's surgery. He told me that Lauren's brain was in the phase of recovery where all the circuits are beginning to light up again and, eventually, they will find ways to re-connect. I was still new to the brain injury world, so I didn't fully understand the meaning of his words. Lauren's new shunt was designed to help regulate her brain fluid levels which was a good thing. Dr. Langdon felt it would help speed up her recovery.

I was hopeful.

Dave and I had been calling and texting each other all morning. Dave took a new job about a year before the accident. It wasn't a good fit and he was miserable. His boss had been understanding with Lauren's accident, but was a tyrant with all work-related issues. Dave had a meeting that morning with his boss. After they finished discussing work issues, his boss asked how Lauren was doing? Dave mentioned that she was currently undergoing brain surgery and he was waiting for me to call with an update. I don't know what came over this typically heartless human, but he suddenly understood how hard it must have been for Dave to show up to work day in and day out with everything going on with Lauren. He suggested Dave take a leave of absence. He assured him his job would be waiting for him when he was ready to return. Dave was on the next plane to Chicago. So many times throughout our marriage I have felt lucky to be his wife, but never more fortunate than when he walked through the threshold of that dreary hospital room. He might as well have been on a white horse, because at that very second, he felt like my knight in shining armor.

Chapter Eight

REHAB IS TOUGH

auren earned an extra day in the hospital; they found a small brain bleed. It's funny how now I felt like a small brain bleed wasn't really much of a big deal. Not funny ha ha, but funny as in odd. Who would have thought I would be like, *Oh, she has a small brain bleed, no big deal.*

Dr. Langdon too felt it wasn't anything to be concerned about but ordered a new CT scan for the next morning. Provided the bleeding stopped, we would be discharged.

I was anxious to get back to RIC. Some of the nurses at Northwestern seemed unsure how to care for Lauren. Most of Lauren's medications were given through her feeding tube. One was given orally to help prevent a fungal infection called thrush. You'd dip a sponge in the medication and then swipe all areas of Lauren's tongue and mouth. The nurse caring for Lauren was at a loss. She stood next to Lauren's bed and asked her to open her mouth several times before I could finally explain to her that Lauren couldn't understand her or follow commands. It felt like Lauren's deficits were multiplied by a thousand while we were at Northwestern.

Earlier that morning, someone from radiology came to get Lauren for her CT scan. Twenty minutes later they brought her back upstairs. I heard them just outside the door talking to her nurse. Listening to them made me sad and angry at the same time. The person from radiology said, "We were unable to administer the test. The patient couldn't follow simple commands. We tried several times, but she didn't seem to understand."

This was about the time I jumped up, opened the door, and said, "So, you decided it would be best to bring her back upstairs without a CT scan. Should we just take a guess as to whether or not her brain is still bleeding?"

The girl looked at me kind of startled and embarrassed, then mumbled something about asking her manager. She wheeled Lauren back into the room and awkwardly walked away. Fifteen minutes later a different girl came upstairs asking me to come along and help position Lauren during the CT scan. I was happy to help.

The first thing they had to confirm was that *I* wasn't pregnant. *Wouldn't that be fun.*

I gave them the short version. "There is no chance that I could be pregnant."

I spared them the truth that four years ago I couldn't jump without peeing on myself and went to see my doctor. Apparently when you spend more than half your adult life pregnant, this is common. My doctor referred me to a bladder surgeon but mentioned that I would also need a partial hysterectomy. He gently explained that my uterus was sliding out of place and it would need to be removed in order for the surgeon to get to my bladder. I thought to myself, *You have no idea how much courage it took for me to come in here and tell you that I couldn't jump without peeing on myself. I never thought you would come back with, "Sure, that can be fixed, but first we need to yank out your uterus, no worries, the good news is that its already falling out."*

So, there I was, standing by the CT machine wearing a lead apron, feeling like I had the weight of the world on my shoulders, literally. I could barely stand upright. I was willing to do whatever was needed so I could get the heck out of this hospital. It was surprisingly simple to hold Lauren still and in the correct position for the CT scan. We were back upstairs twenty minutes later. By this time, I was tired of waiting on tests and waiting on doctors and waiting on discharge; I was starting to lose it.

I was frustrated, exhausted, and for the very first time since the accident, I was angry and I realized I was angry at Lauren. I had spent the last sixty plus days sitting in a chair staring at a child who had no clue who I was. Two months ago, I had a job that I loved, a life that was easy, a happy marriage, a happy house, everything except the picket fence. I wanted to scream, "Why did you run out in front of a car! Do you see what this has done to my life?"

I was tired of cold hospital rooms, bad coffee, and no sleep. I wanted my old life back; I was tired, and I didn't know if I could keep doing this. Thankfully we soon received word that the CT scans were good, and we were being discharged. Dave had arrived and life was looking up. When the discharge paperwork was taking forever, Dave looked at me and said, "I got this. Go back to the apartment and take a nap. We will be fine."

I was reluctant but knew I needed to go.

Back at my apartment I couldn't sleep. I was mad at myself for being mad at Lauren. She didn't ask for this. No matter how hard this was for me, it was much worse for her. Once again, I felt like I was the grand prize winner of the Worst Mother in the World Award. What kind of selfish witch turns their daughter's tragedy into being about herself? I took a shower to rid myself of the hospital smell so I could prepare myself for the *other* hospital smell.

While Lauren was still at Northwestern, we received word that she had C-Diff. C-Diff is a bacterial infection in the colon. It causes stomach pain and frequent foul-smelling bouts of diarrhea. All diarrhea is foul smelling, but C-Diff is in a category all on its own. Lauren was having several bowel movements a day so I knew I couldn't be gone long; Dave was too nice to people to be the one making sure Lauren doesn't sit in poop too long. I wasn't mean but I was demanding. It would have been weird for Dave to have changed Lauren's diapers; it was never an option. I knew Lauren would have hated it more than having a stranger do it. Besides, Dave had probably only changed ten to twenty diapers in his entire life. Kind of unfair, if you ask me. He has seven children, barely changed any diapers, and you don't see any of *his* vital organs falling out.

Now that Dave was on a leave of absence from work, the only people in the household with jobs were Shannon and Kelsey. They worked at a little ice cream shop making a few cents an hour over minimum wage. We often joked that those two were solely responsible for keeping the family afloat. When Dave was with me in Chicago it meant the kids were at home without a parent. We tried hard to keep a balance. I loved it when Dave or the kids were with me, but they had to maintain a sense of normalcy at home and I had to establish a routine at RIC.

One thing I started doing first thing every morning for Lauren was to become her personal makeup artist. There wasn't a whole heck of a lot I could do to help her. I knew her appearance was important, so I did the best I could. Every morning I came armed with a whole bag of tricks, including eyeliner, mascara, perfume, and jewelry. One time when I was applying her makeup, Lauren picked up a lipstick and started putting more on. From then on, I made sure she always had fresh lipstick. Every morning, before Jim would come to get her for physical therapy, I would often say, "Hold on a second, she needs fresh lipstick."

I think Jim thought I was crazy. Actually I *know* he thought I was crazy. I explained to him that lipstick was a "game changer." I don't think they taught that in PT school, but I believed that maybe they should have. I would also put hair product in the little bit of hair that had grown back. Her recent surgery added a horseshoe shaped scar on the right side of her head. She also still had over a dozen staples, which all in all made styling her hair a bit of a challenge.

Erin came to visit for the Fourth of July holiday. Lauren had recovered well from surgery and was back to working hard in all of her therapies. On July 3, we were walking the halls with Jim during a normal PT session. Lauren was doing well but still struggled with balance, her sense of center was way off, which prevented her from walking on her own. Her attention span was another issue. She would stop and try to turn every door knob, touch every laundry cart, and basically focus on everything *except* the task at hand. We had just made our first lap around the unit when I noticed something was off. Lauren's feet quit moving forward and her face looked amiss. It was hard to put my finger on it; she still wasn't showing emotion or facial expressions, but my mother's intuition was in overdrive.

It began with a curl in her lip, and then her eye began to twitch. She made a face that looked unnatural. It almost reminded me of someone who was trying not to cry, their facial muscles contorting in a crying stance while the person tries to close their mouth or force their facial expression into neutral. The whole right side of Lauren's face started curling up into a very unnatural muscle spasm set of contractions. Her eyes were blinking, and her eyeballs were rolling back in her head as her head trembled. I turned to Jim and asked, "Is she having a seizure?"

Jim, who was super laid back and calm, quietly said, "I think so, yes."

No sooner did he get those words out, Lauren's body began to convulse violently. Jim and I were trying to get her back in her wheelchair when the convulsions began. I was behind her and could not lower her into her chair now that she was convulsing, her legs were too stiff. Jim called for a nurse and a gurney, the nurses were scrambling to get the gurney as well as medication. As I held Lauren under her shoulders, I asked Jim, "What am I supposed to do?"

I felt so helpless. I had never seen a seizure, much less tried to hold someone up during one. Faint moaning noises were coming from Lauren, which was really hard, she had not made a single sound for months. Even through her moans, I could tell that it was her voice. I had longed to hear her voice, but not like this. *This* was awful. While all was happening, I looked over at Erin, who was pushed up against the wall, her face bright red from crying. My heart was broken. I had *two* children who needed help, yet I could only help one. And the saddest part was that I wasn't even helping. All I could do was wait for the seizure to stop.

Shortly after the gurney arrived, a team of people scooped her up, and someone administered medication rectally to help stop the seizure. They wheeled her back to her room with her pants still at her ankles. I felt like her dignity had been violated, yet I wasn't mad. There is no time for modesty during an emergency and I was impressed with how quickly they responded. It just made me sad. Lauren looked so vulnerable and broken, I remember feeling like this nightmare was never going to end.

When things calmed down, I noticed her diamond necklace, her sparkly earrings and her freshly applied bright pink lipstick. I felt like an idiot. Ten minutes ago, I thought those things made a difference, now I thought they were making me look like a shallow moron. Dr. Ballard arrived rather quickly; the decision was made to put Lauren on an anti-seizure medication right away. He asked us to try and spend the rest of the week low key and quiet. Overstimulation could be a trigger for seizures. Jim came by her room later in the day to apologize. "I'm sorry that happened during therapy," he said.

My heart broke for Jim. I could tell how bad he felt that it happened on his watch. When I first met Jim, I remember being unsure, he was really quiet and wasn't bubbling over with personality.

I remember the exact moment that my view of Jim changed.

A few weeks after we arrived at RIC, all of Lauren's doctors and therapists got together to go over Lauren's assessments, as well as care plan for her time there. Dave and I sat around a table as Dr. Ballard directed the meeting. The news was not rosy. This was the first time I had heard the word "aphasia." Dr. Ballard explained that because Lauren had had the language portion of her brain removed, she was incapable of understanding spoken words and would always struggle with finding her words. He felt that her right arm would always be spastic, and she would never regain its full use. Walking was not in the cards. They intended to work on what was called "stand and pivot." If Lauren can learn to shift her weight, transferring her to the wheelchair and bed would be much easier. In speech we were hoping to get her to swallow clear liquids on a spoon and work toward a better attention span. This seemed to be a common problem for all the therapists. She could not pay attention to anything or anyone. I wanted to stand up and tell them to shut up. I intended for my daughter to walk, talk, and use her arm again. They had set the bar too low. We are Murphys and Murphys don't quit!

After the meeting Dave was sad and said, "It is what it is."

I knew they were wrong, and Dave and I had to agree to disagree.

The next day, while Lauren was walking on the treadmill in a harness, Jim looked at me and said, "What did you think of the meeting?"

I was surprised he asked because Jim was usually so quiet and reserved. I decided to be brutally honest. "I thought it was BS. She *is* going to get better!"

He chuckled and told me that he has seen several miracles at RIC and, yes, to keep the faith. That was the exact moment that I knew Jim was a keeper.

The rest of the week Erin and I basically sat around and watched Lauren sleep. When she was awake, she was lethargic. The seizure seemed to really set her back. They told me that the new medication would make her tired, but I wasn't expecting this. Several days later I was still watching Lauren sit in her wheelchair struggling to hold her head up. We had come so far, and one stupid seizure erased weeks and weeks of progress.

I spoke with one of the doctors on the team. He was an intern. I asked him about taking her off the anti-seizure medication. She was like a zombie—certainly dealing with seizures would be better than this heavily medicated version of Lauren. He seemed to like my idea and said he would talk to Dr. Ballard. Minutes later I was shot down. I knew not to argue. He used to be a redhead, and I didn't think my expired cosmetology license gave me much clout arguing against his medical degree. They assured me she would eventually adjust to the medication, and they were right.

Lauren continued to throw up a lot. Her tube feedings didn't agree with her. There was a washer and dryer on the floor, but I always took her dirty clothes home with me. I liked to be able to use Tide and Downy Unstoppables so everything would smell like home. Every night I would carry her soiled wet clothes and blankets home in one of those plastic hospital belongings bag. The handle was similar to kite string. It would twist around my wrist as I walked, cutting off my circulation, not the most comfortable way to carry wet clothes home. As a Catholic, I was always taught to offer it up. I remember thinking on one of my walks home, *I keep offering up my suffering, yet here I am carrying heavy vomit- and poop-covered clothes again. Anyone out there listening?*

Some nights my short walk back to my apartment was agonizing. I would pass several restaurants with patio seating. The sounds of happy people enjoying a dinner with friends or family or dates made me mad with jealousy. I was tired of going home to a silent empty apartment. Many nights I cried out to God. I would shout the same prayer over and over again. "Please fix her, help me fix her. Dear God, I need you to show me how to fix her."

I have always been someone of faith, but I am not one who feels comfortable praying aloud. This was way out of my comfort zone. I wasn't just praying aloud, I was wailing in complete anguish, desperation, and grief. Lucky for me I had the whole floor to myself. Otherwise I might have scared the neighbors.

Chapter Nine

PREPARING FOR DISCHARGE

L auren's room overlooked Lake Michigan. Just outside her window you could see an area known as "The Playpen." One of the nurses explained this was where people came to party. There must have been over a hundred boats anchored out there on any given day. We have something similar called "Party Cove" at a lake near our house. Party Cove is a little crazy; I suspected The Playpen was the same.

The old Lauren would have been out there with them, looking for the biggest party. She was like her mom when it came to worshiping the sun. Unlike her mom, she also enjoyed hanging out on boats and day drinking. I was happy to have a room with a view, but I was sad for yet another reminder of what she was missing.

For her first semester of college, Lauren lived in Chicago. She wanted to study fashion and her hope was to go somewhere in New York, Chicago, or Los Angeles. Considering we couldn't even afford to do a college visit as far away as New York or Los Angeles, she settled on Chicago. When we came up to look at colleges, I should have recognized the red flags. We spent more time shopping on Michigan Avenue then we did tour college campuses. We did, however, come home with a gorgeous blue-beaded prom dress.

I knew Lauren would be unhappy going to school in Chicago, but I also knew that she had to figure it out on her own. Despite her aspirations, she was the type of kid that didn't like to be away from home.

A few weeks before she left for college, Lauren found a lump in her breast. Thankfully it was benign, but the surgeon felt it needed to come out. Lauren had a lumpectomy the week before she left. The timing was terrible; she was anxious about leaving home and now had to worry about changing her dressings and keeping incisions clean while showering in a bathroom shared with her whole dorm floor. After her summer orientation she confessed that she wasn't sure about her choice, but because of that whole "Murphys don't quit" thing, she knew she had to follow through with it, at least for the first semester.

Move-in day was miserable. Her roommate was there with her parents and they were all upbeat and super excited. In sharp contrast, Lauren was acting like she was at a funeral. We decided to go to Target to pick out a few things for the room. I wasn't overly thrilled about our Target trip—in those days money was super tight. Lauren moped around from aisle to aisle, while I got more and more annoyed as we put things we couldn't afford in our cart. I lost it when I asked her to pick out an alarm clock (this was before iPhones), and she looked at me all depressed and said, "I guess this one is fine."

She didn't even look at the selection. She was acting like such a Debbie Downer. That was when I went into psycho mom mode. "Pick out an alarm clock, put it in the cart, and stop acting like an ungrateful brat. Your dad and I can't even afford this stuff, and you are acting like you are dying. *You* made the choice to go to this school. You are absolutely not coming home and lying on our couch for a semester. Make the best of it and start looking at options for the spring."

At that very moment I realized that maybe the middle of Target was not the best place for my little tantrum. (Surely there was a Walmart in town.) Dave pulled me aside after my little outburst. "I don't think you are helping the situation," he said.

What an idiot. When will he ever learn to just be quiet and keep his stupid opinions to himself?

Now I wondered, had she stayed in Chicago for all four years of college, would she have spent a few weekends at the *Playpen*? I'm pretty sure she would have.

I was happy that at RIC, despite the doctor's prognosis, they seemed to do everything within their power to try and help Lauren. She was receiving Botox in her right arm and a series of casts to try to both loosen and straighten her arm. (After the summer I was having, I knew that I would soon be needing Botox more than she did.) Once we finished the series of casts, she had to wear a custom-made brace to keep her arm straight. There was nothing physically wrong with her arm; the connections in her brain were not getting to her arm to signal movement. If we didn't continue to stimulate her arm and keep it straight, her arm would return to its previous position stuck against her chest. I was not about to let that happen.

Lauren was becoming feistier, which was good. I knew that keeping a brace on her at night would be tricky. She still had to wear those big Prafo boots when she slept and now we were adding a bulky brace that covered the whole length of her right arm. Many mornings I would come in and find her brace off and down at the foot of her bed. When I asked, her nurses would always say, "Sorry, she takes it off at night."

I would try to find a way to tactfully say, "Sorry, you need to put it back on her at night."

It was very important for that brace to stay on for long periods of time. During therapy it was hard, but while she slept it was important. Eventually I realized that unless I stayed with her all night to keep watch, I would get the same result. Thankfully, Murphys don't quit so I found a way to keep it on. I put sweatpants (that were tight at the ankle) over her arm, then took the drawstring from the waist and wrapped it all around her arm with several knots. There was no way she would get that brace off now.

Had that not worked, I was prepared to go to the store to buy duct tape.

Lauren still wasn't talking but had started mouthing words, like *hi, how are you, good morning etc.* Doctors explained that she was able to come up with things that were automatic, but words that required her brain to process and think were still lost to her. I get the whole *not wanting to give false hope* scenario, but every once in a while, I would have loved to hear a doctor say, "That is so awesome. Keep up the great work."

One day Lauren leaned into Dave and gave him a kiss on the cheek. I was like, *Seriously, he shows up, and five minutes later he gets a kiss?* I had flashbacks to when the kids were little and every time he walked in the front door after a long day at work they acted as if he was the second coming of Christ. She would eventually give me kisses too, and every once in a while, she would even give me a smile. I was thrilled. I felt like she was working her way back to us.

Back at home, Dave had made the first steps in hiring a contractor to make our house handicap accessible. Lauren's balance was getting better, and she was getting closer to walking. I had been putting her on the toilet several times a day. Her constant C-Diff was actually helping our success rate. That said, it was much easier potty training her the first time around. I was hoping she would master the toilet quickly. I resorted back to my old ways; I would sing songs, and instead of bringing in childhood books and M&M's, we had a stack of *People* magazines and bottles of Ensure.

Eating was not going well. Thankfully, she didn't have any issues with swallowing, she just didn't like the texture of food. I would order pancakes and have to feed her bites that were so small they were basically just syrup on a fork. Most foods she would spit out the second I gave her a bite.

I didn't know it at the time, but Lauren lost her sense of smell and taste in the accident. This made trying to get her to eat very challenging. Texture was a big deal for her without taste. She was unable to communicate this to us for a very long time. Once I was able to confirm that she lost her sense of smell (over a year later), the first thing I thought of was all those nights I struggled to carry her heavy wet clothes to my apartment. I felt it was imperative that her stuff smelled like home, not a hospital. Come to find out, the girl can't even smell—one of the many stupid things I have done along this journey. Once I was able to transport her to her wheelchair from her bed, another dumb thing I would do was if she took what *I felt* was too many naps, I would pick her up, put her in her wheelchair and say, "Nobody gets better sleeping."

I would take her for a walk around the unit in her wheelchair or stick an iPad in front of her to try and make her watch YouTube videos, anything to keep her stimulated and awake. (A few years later I read an article about how important it was for patients to get extra sleep during their recovery. Whoops! Sorry Lauren.)

The time was coming for us to start thinking about discharge. A woman from another brain injury facility in Omaha, Nebraska came to talk to me about Lauren going there for the next phase of her recovery. One of the first things she did was ask Lauren, "Do you understand what has happened to you?"

Lauren nodded *yes*.

I almost fell out of my chair. I had no clue she knew anything that was going on. I liked this lady; she knew how to talk to Lauren and include her in the conversation. She talked about her facility and how it was set up like a college for brain injury. It was a great place for independence. I agreed that it looked like a great place, but I was not interested at this time. I wanted to go home.

The kind woman looked at me said, "Can I ask why you feel like this isn't the best option?"

"I have an eleven-year-old."

She must have been a mother because with that, she packed up her brochures, gave me a warm smile, and wished us luck. In the prior four months I had only seen my youngest two kids two or three times. I felt extremely out of the loop and needed to go back home. My older kids needed me just as much as the little ones, if not more. I had been gone long enough.

Our whole family shared a phone plan as well as one iTunes account. The year 2013 was similar to the Dark Ages in regard to iPhone technology. I soon learned (the hard way) that the latest iPhone update had a bit of a glitch. I was sitting in Lauren's room on a typical Saturday morning, waiting for one of her scheduled therapists, when my phone rang. It was a FaceTime call meant for Erin's phone that crossed over to my number. I answered the call and saw Erin's boyfriend shirtless. I hung up as quickly as possible. *Oh god, was he naked? Or did he just have his shirt off?* I hoped he just had his shirt off. Why would he be FaceTiming Erin naked, or with his shirt off?

I really didn't want to know the answer.

A few hours later I was part of a group text with all of Shannon's friends. They were planning to go to dinner at a restaurant called El Maguey. I learned from the text that apparently they don't card, and underage drinking is a given. Who knew? I was happy to get the phone situation fixed but was starting to second-guess myself. Did I really want to go back home to all those delinquents?

RIC was preparing us for life at home, not with naked boyfriends and underage drinking, but with learning to take over all of Lauren's care. My caregiver sheet on her closet door was full of checkmarks. Full disclosure, I started checking the boxes on my own. Dave would have never dreamed of checking off boxes himself; he has always been such a rule follower. But I knew the quicker those boxes were checked, the quicker we were going home. Besides, I can't even remember the last person who looked at my caregiver sheet. Maybe they were scared of me because of all the times I went a little crazy over the little things like her schedule not being correct, or my personal favorite, finding poop under her fingernails morning after morning. I remember a specific conversation I had with a nurse after the third or fourth time this happened. Our chat went something like this:

> **ME**: *How long must have she been left sitting in a soiled diaper for her to have poop under her fingernails?*
> **NURSE**: *I'm sorry. I will make sure to note it in her chart for the night shift.*
> **ME**: *If you have to put a note in her chart to let them know that they shouldn't let her sit in poop for too long, we have a problem.*

I had taken over most of Lauren's care as soon as I was able. I gave her all of her showers, helped her dress, and brushed her teeth each day, I cheered her on for each and every bite of food and, of course, I made sure her lipstick was always fresh. I had all of the important things covered. Lauren was always red carpet ready. I couldn't remember the last time I shaved my legs, but hers were shaved at least every other day. The only thing I didn't do was administer her medication.

As the days turned into weeks, I knew I would have to make a hard decision in regard to my job. My hopes were that her shunt surgery was going to make such a difference in her recovery that I would be able to return to work. I was really proud of my career and loved my job, but I loved my daughter more. I knew that Lauren needed me. On July 18th, I called my boss and sent in my letter of resignation:

> *It is with a very heavy heart that at the end of my leave I have no other choice but to resign. Lauren has made great strides, but the healing pro-*

cess is a long one. It could be 6 months to a year before she is able to live more independently. Cognitively she is just not with us yet. As a mother I cannot in good conscience return to work and let nursing staff take care of Lauren.

I had tears in my eyes as I wrote that letter, not only because I was sad to be leaving a job that I loved but also because I felt like I was giving up on Lauren. If I truly believed she would recover, I could have extended my leave of absence, but I didn't.

We were located downtown, deep in the heart of Cubs country. Lauren's room had a STL Cardinals poster on the outside of her door, commemorating the years—all eleven of them—of World Series wins. Most people upon entering, commented on how they hated our poster, probably because the Cubs had yet to win a World Series to overcome the "Billy Goat Curse," which incidentally involved a goat named Murphy. During one of my conversations with staff, we were joking about the Cards/Cubs rivalry, and I told them if Lauren was able to learn to walk by her discharge date, I would dress her in a Chicago Cubs t-shirt for her discharge. They took me up on the deal.

I knew without a doubt that she would be walking out of there in a Cubs shirt. Dave wasn't as optimistic and always tried to protect me by saying things like, "I don't want you to get your hopes up."

I would just tell him he was stupid, and he wasn't seeing what I was seeing. It's amazing how miles apart we could still annoy each other. My neighbor had the perfect Cubs shirt for us. Jim Edmonds was a STL Cardinal for seven seasons until traded to the Cubs. He was always a fan favorite. If Lauren was going to wear a Cubs jersey, it seemed fitting to have a famous St. Louis Cardinal's name on the back.

Lauren's discharge date finally arrived on August 24, 2013. It was the day after Rick Springfield's sixty-fourth birthday—not that that fun fact mattered to anyone other than myself, but it did make it easier for me to remember her discharge date.

On August 13, Lauren took thirty-seven steps during a PT session with Jim. We couldn't believe it. I was taping per usual and caught the whole thing on film;

otherwise I would have had no clue it was exactly thirty-seven steps. Thankfully I am the forever stage mom. I knew she could and would do it! I was so proud of her and I was so thankful that RIC paired her with Jim.

While we were working on walking in Chicago, Dave and the kids worked on getting a temporary room set up for Lauren in our dining room. The hospital bed had just been delivered. We moved into our current house when Lauren was in college, so she never had a bedroom at our new house. The dining room "bedroom" would be temporary. Construction on our house was scheduled to start in mid-September.

Dave arrived back in Chicago on Rick's birthday; we were super excited to go home.

I was not super excited when he told me that he had forgotten the Jim Edmonds t-shirt. Seriously? I was annoyed but figured we could just run by Target in the morning to pick up a Cubs t-shirt before discharge. I had been talking to Lauren and telling her over the last several days that we were going home. I had no clue if she understood, but I hoped that she did. The night before, I packed up all of her stuff and loaded it in our rental SUV. I decided to wait until the next morning to take down all of the room decor, as I didn't want Lauren to wake up to a dreary room. Dave thought I was crazy. Was he just now figuring this out?

The next morning, Dave and I stopped at Target to grab a Cubs shirt. Imagine my surprise that Target didn't have a single Cubs shirt in stock. *Your home team is so bad they don't even have t-shirts in August? The season is still going on!*

We settled on a Chicago Bears t-shirt; I was annoyed with Dave all over again for forgetting the Edmonds shirt. Sometimes I feel like I should pin notes to the front of his shirt like they do in kindergarten. How did he forget the one thing I needed from home?

When we arrived at RIC, Lauren seemed happy. I felt like she knew she was going home. I don't know how to describe it, but I could definitely see it in her eyes. Maybe because I had spent over four months staring into her eyes, and normally all I could see was blankness. I could tell that today was different. She seemed to be more aware.

At 127 days after her accident, she was finally going home!

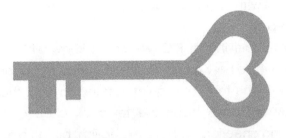

Key 2: Find Your Cheerleader

f I were to ask, who is your biggest cheerleader? Without a doubt, I'd say a mental picture of someone appears. As kids, our parents were our biggest cheerleaders. They encouraged us from the sidelines of our sporting events, dance recitals, academic achievements, and graduations. As we get older, our cheerleading network grows, often adding our close friends, significant others, and coworkers.

My favorite cheerleader is my husband Dave. Shortly after we met, he became the first person I called when I had news to share. My girlfriends are still pretty high up on the list, but Dave is, without a doubt, my head cheerleader. A perfect example would be when he walked through the door at Northwestern University Hospital after Lauren's fourth brain surgery. Despite me telling him I had things under control, he knew in his heart that I didn't. We all need a cheerleader that knows what we need, even if we can't see it for ourselves.

Lauren has been blessed with dozens of cheerleaders throughout her recovery. The first is Dr. Chen. What would I have done in those early days back at Cedars without the positive energy and enthusiasm of Dr. Chen! Next, was Lauren's friend, Courtney. She filled Lauren's ICU room with so much hope and optimism, a gift I needed and can never repay.

Weeks later, arriving at RIC, we didn't know what to expect. We welcomed a whole new group of cheerleaders. My favorite RIC cheerleader came in the form of a quiet, gentle, physical therapist named Jim. He may not have been the textbook cheery, bubbly, megaphone-carrying cheerleader I was expecting, but he sure came up big when it looked as if no one else shared my enthusiasm.

Coming out of nowhere was the male nurse at Northwestern Hospital who gave me that much needed hug. Giving hugs wasn't part of his job description, yet he knew I desperately needed to hear that I was doing a good job.

Finding your cheerleader during times of triumph is easy; everyone wants to be your friend when life is glorious. Finding your cheerleader during the tough times proves to be a bit more challenging. Don't be afraid to ask for help!

Chapter Ten

HOME SWEET HOME

The drive home from Chicago was fairly uneventful. We stopped at a gas station before we hit St. Louis to change Lauren out of the ugly blue and orange Chicago Bears t-shirt. She would be coming home in a STL Cardinals t-shirt and a little black running skirt.

Our ride home wouldn't be considered uneventful by most standards, but because I am a Murphy, I am used to things not always going as planned. Murphy's Law states "Anything that can go wrong, will go wrong." Since I've been married to Dave, I can pretty much agree with the authentic nature of Murphy's Law. None of this crazy stuff happened before he swept me off my feet with his boyish charm, taped together glasses, and bright blue 1978 Camaro with a broken door handle. If that alone didn't impress me, the Budweiser bottle caps he attached to his car stereo knobs pretty much sealed the deal. I reeled in quite the catch!

We were about an hour outside Chicago when I realized the discharge nurse forgot to give me a syringe to administer Lauren's medicine. I had the pill crusher, bottle of water, and plastic cup, but no syringe. And I needed a specific type of syringe that fit in her feeding tube. We stopped in a small-town Walmart. Dave went in to talk to the pharmacist, who didn't have anything like that in stock but recommended a small pharmacy on the other side of town.

Dave drove to the pharmacy, went in to ask, then came back to the car and asked me to go inside and talk to them. They didn't have the type I needed but they had something similar that could possibly work. The only problem was that we had to buy the whole box. I didn't care what it cost, I only had about an hour to either teach her how to swallow pills or find a syringe. $150 dollars later, we were back on the road with a box of two hundred plastic syringes.

I sat in the backseat with Lauren on the ride home, recalling when I rode in the back next to her when she was a baby coming home for the first time from the hospital. Her little head kept falling forward in the rear-facing car seat. I was worried it would hurt her neck, so I held my hand on her forehead the whole way home to keep her upright. I now would often think of Lauren's recovery like pregnancy and childhood. Her first trimester was similar to her early ICU days. Her second trimester was when she emerged from her coma and began to focus. The third trimester was her getting stronger for the move to Chicago. The time at RIC was a rebirth for Lauren; she had to relearn everything like she did as an infant. I tried to look at the positive. I was falling in love with her all over again. How many mothers got to raise their children twice?

I received a do-over.

One thing I knew for sure was that I would teach her a strong appreciation for Rick Springfield. The old Lauren never gave him the respect that he so obviously deserved.

I had been texting with the kids during the drive home, so they knew when to expect us. 5 minutes from our house I noticed a huge banner on the highway overpass that read, MURPHY STRONG. My heart was full.

My daughter Kelsey hung the "Murphy Strong" banner. To describe her in one word, I would have to say "extra." She is the type of kid that goes "all in" on everything that she does. Unfortunately, her huge heart does not line up with her tiny bank account. She sees a need and jumps right in to help, whether it be volunteering for twenty-five committees at school, or just collecting money to help people in times of crisis. Her heart is always open. I am proud of how hard she works to help others, but what I don't like is that when she comes up short in donations, she gets the rest of the money from me. I didn't realize what a great humanitarian I was until Kelsey began trying to save the world. She isn't afraid to get out there and be bold. She is a lot like Lauren in that aspect.

Kelsey took charge of arranging Lauren's homecoming party. We had to be careful not to overstimulate Lauren upon arriving home, but also wanted to mark this occasion with something special. So many people had followed our story and sent prayers, gifts, food, and love that we wanted to share this moment with them. I firmly believe that all of their prayers and support helped get us to where we were.

The original plan was to have a few friends and neighbors outside cheering us on as Lauren arrived home. I should have known that Kelsey, along with the rest of the Murphy kids, would turn it into something completely over the top. Kelsey and Maggie went to every single house in our neighborhood and put fliers in mailboxes, and Sam had posted the homecoming information on Lauren's CaringBridge site. I knew we would have a good-size crowd, but I never could have imagined how big it truly was.

When we pulled down our street, I couldn't believe my eyes. Both sides of the street were lined with over two hundred people—neighbors, sports teams, friends, and family. A fire truck was parked out front with a huge *Murphy's Don't Quit* sign covering the whole left side, directly under the big ladder. Never in my wildest dreams could I have imagined so much love when we came home. I briefly considered getting out of the car, getting on my hands and knees and kissing the driveway like the Pope when he gets off an airplane. I was *that* happy to be home.

Everyone gathered around for a quick picture. As we stood for a tight group photo, Lauren recognized Vicki, one of our neighbors from our previous neighborhood. When Lauren was younger, she would dog sit for Vicki, who always stocked her fridge with orange juice just for Lauren. That was their little inside joke. When Lauren saw Vicki, her whole face lit up. I immediately started crying. To see her recognize someone she didn't see on a regular basis, someone from her childhood, was huge.

We took our group picture and headed inside. I left the wheelchair in the back of the car. It was important for me to have her walk, not be wheeled through the front door.

Later that evening Lauren was lying in my bed surrounded by all of her siblings. "I'm happy," Lauren softly said.

We all pretty much melted upon hearing her words. And her words were not a whisper, they were audible, real words. Her voice was softer and a little scratchy, but it was still *her* voice. Many times I wondered if I would ever hear her voice again. Nothing could have possibly sounded any sweeter at that exact moment than those two words.

Erin came home from college for Lauren's homecoming and was headed back to Alabama the next evening. She agreed to sleep on the couch next to Lauren's hospital bed that first night. I was happy to take her up on her offer, as I had only slept in my bed one night in the last four months.

The next morning. Erin woke up to the sound of our front window blinds shaking. She looked up and Lauren was standing at the window looking outside. I can only assume that Lauren woke up confused as to where she was. I could also assume that Erin was now fired from keeping watch. Lauren was still not real steady on her feet and couldn't walk without someone being right next to her. Her hospital bed came equipped with an alarm that would sound if she got out of bed, but we didn't set the alarm that first night, thinking if someone was with her they would hear her waking up. This was one of her many silent ninja type escapades yet to come.

While we were still at RIC, I set up Lauren's outpatient therapy in St. Louis to begin the Monday after we arrived home. I wanted her to get right to work to keep the momentum going. The kids had all started school the week before, so our mornings were back to the crazy chaos of looking for matching socks (we still never had enough socks), packing lunches, grabbing a Pop-Tart and heading out the door. I remember thinking, *This really sucks. Why did I miss this?*

I got Lauren's stuff ready for therapy the night before. Our morning routine included, of course, hair and makeup, along with crushing her pills, mixing them with water, and giving them to her with a syringe via her feeding tube. I also had to allow enough time for her morning tube feed. I made sure I packed enough diapers, wipes (she had been doing well on the toilet, but I wanted to be prepared), and afternoon meds, plus bags of tube feeding to last throughout the day. I felt like I was packing her diaper bag for the babysitter all over again. I was never this organized when my kids were little. By the time I got to my fourth or fifth kid, I never even bothered packing a diaper bag. I spent the majority of my time away from home at a sports practice or game. Organized diaper bags were no longer on my radar. When I needed it, there was usually an extra diaper under the seat of our van.

Lauren's new therapy facility was thirty-five miles away. I was hoping to be a little early, as I wasn't sure how much traffic we would encounter. Since I drove a little Honda Accord, Lauren's wheel chair had to be taken apart to fit in the trunk. Thankfully she no longer had the hot pink, lime green combo. In its place, she had a custom-made powder blue, lightweight, spiffy new wheelchair.

That morning, I got in my car ready to start the next leg of Lauren's recovery. It felt good to get behind the wheel of a car again. I had not driven a car since we left Los Angeles and I hadn't driven *my* car since the day I got that awful phone call that changed everything. I started the engine and backed out of the driveway. A few yards down the road I glanced at my gas gauge. The light was on and it showed, *two miles to empty.* This was the exact moment that my head spun all the way around, and I began to spew green vomit like Linda Blair in *The Exorcist.*

I dialed Kelsey's phone number. Turns out Kelsey had been too busy driving all over town hanging "Murphy Strong" banners and dropping off fliers, she failed to fill up my tank on her way home. This was more proof that Dave and I should have stopped having kids at the national average of 2.2 instead of 7.0. After some quick Google research, I found out that in the year 2013 the average number of children per family had dropped down to 1.8. Who knew? That just made us even more stupid than I had originally thought.

After ten Hail Marys I miraculously made it to the gas station without running out of gas. I filled up my tank and merged onto the highway. Thirty seconds later, Lauren was covered in vomit, and not the imaginary *Exorcist* vomit, but the real-life soaked through her clothes, all down the side of my car kind. I turned around at the next exit, called to let the facility know we would be late, and headed home for dry clothes.

An hour later we were signing in at the front desk for therapy.

Before Lauren and I started therapy that morning, we met with the director of the program, who asked Lauren what college she had attended. I was waiting for her typical response of *Good morning.* Instead, she said, "Bachelor of Science, Fashion Merchandising."

I almost fell over. Even though it was the wrong answer, she was on the right track. Two days earlier she was whispering pleasantries, and now she was saying real words.

Her new speech therapist was great. She explained to me what it had to be like for Lauren. She used the analogy of a hurricane coming through a library, shelves knocked over, books scattered on the floor, some books rain soaked and damaged, others okay but in the wrong section. She explained that for Lauren, learning to speak again is similar to that hurricane. She needs to start working on sorting through the rubble, one day at a time.

Later that evening I shared the story of the hurricane analogy along with the rest of Lauren's therapy highlights with my brother-in-law, Jim.

"She's on the right chapter," he said, "she just has the wrong page."

He was so right, and I was once again hopeful for a future that included Lauren possibly speaking again.

I knew coming home would be wonderful, but it also presented many new challenges. Lauren's beauty regimen didn't stop now that we were home. Each week I painted her nails and kept her eyebrows perfectly plucked. I wanted her to feel as much like the old Lauren as possible. Showering Lauren at our house was a big challenge. I was anxiously waiting for her handicap shower to be installed. In the meantime, I had to awkwardly stand outside the shower with Lauren either sitting in a shower chair or standing while I held her up with my right hand (my strongest arm) and used my left hand to wash her skin and hair or shave her legs and armpits. If that wasn't challenging enough, with the shower door open, water sprayed all over me. Once finished, I would get her dressed while my own clothes were soaked. Thankfully, construction of the newly equipped bathroom was scheduled to start soon. But first we had to select tile and paint and flooring and fixtures. Choosing finishes was actually a nice distraction, as taking care of Lauren full time was hard work, mentally as well as physically.

A week or so after Lauren's homecoming, Dave and I went to look at tile. When we got home that evening, Lauren was in her pajamas ready for bed. I laid down with her for a while and then I too went to bed exhausted. The next morning, as I was getting Lauren's medication ready, I realized I forgot her evening medication the night before. Lauren was eating breakfast as I gave her the belated medicine through her feeding tube. She had just taken a bite of banana when I saw her eyes begin to twitch. I knew what was about to happen, and that it was entirely my fault. *How could I have forgotten her medicine? Was bathroom tile that important?*

Immediately, I reached into her mouth to remove any banana. I held onto her with one hand and dialed 911 with the other. She started to violently shake. All I could do was hold her in place and pray with all my heart that the seizure would soon stop. They normally last less than five minutes, but to me each scary minute felt like hours. This seizure thankfully stopped before EMS arrived. After checking her vitals, EMS agreed with me that a trip the ER was not necessary. They reminded me how important taking medication on time was to prevent seizures. I deserved the scolding. Once again, I felt like the worst mother in the history of the world. I called and canceled her therapy for the day and vowed to be better. I couldn't afford to make mistakes; this was my daughter's life I had in my hands.

———

Lauren's balance was improving. Although we never let her go upstairs without help, she began waking up in the middle of the night, unplugging her bed, and going upstairs to dig through her boxes of clothes and shoes that had been shipped to our house from New York. One of us (Dave) would wake up at 3:00 a.m. and find Lauren dressed in a party dress and heels with fresh lipstick. We bought a baby monitor that detected movement; I would receive a text message on my phone whenever she moved. That would have been a great solution if I wasn't such a heavy sleeper.

So many of my friends tell me that once they became mothers, they became super light sleepers. Unfortunately, that was not the case for me. I think motherhood made me so exhausted I became a *heavier* sleeper. Before Lauren's accident, Kelsey broke her collarbone during a soccer game. The doctor told us that the bone was not broken all the way through and that it would not be uncommon for the rest of the bone to snap in the next couple of days. He was preparing us, just in case it happened. Two nights later, Kelsey rolled over in her bed and felt her collarbone crack. Even though she knew this might happen, it scared her, and it was painful. She came downstairs to wake me up. Regrettably, when I am in the middle of good sleep, I am often like a rabid dog if someone tries to interrupt my perfect slumber. That night was no exception.

Kelsey was crying and very hard to understand. "Mom, I broke my bone."

"What?" I was half asleep and annoyed.

"I broke my bone," she repeated.

"Kelsey, I don't care if you broke your *phone*. It's the middle of the night."

Kelsey cried harder. "My *bone*, Mom. My bone, not my phone. It hurts so bad."

That woke me up 100 percent. "Oh no. I suck. I'm sorry, honey. Let's get you some Advil."

It is safe to say I parent much better during regular business hours. Late-night emergencies are better left for Dave. Now I'm sure my teenagers love that I am such a heavy sleeper, especially all the nights they are late for curfew, probably hanging at the local Mexican restaurants.

Those first few weeks at home, I would wake up to a string of texts from the baby monitor app and wonder what Lauren had been doing all night. One morning I discovered a cookie sheet on the counter with a dozen piping hot biscuits. Lauren somehow woke up, went into the kitchen, got out a cookie sheet, opened a tube of Pillsbury biscuits (I can never open those), turned on the oven, and cooked them to golden brown perfection without anyone in the house hearing a thing.

Lauren also started trying to take her medicine on her own, I think she thought the medicine would help her get better. Although logical, not true. I found her one day drinking her liquid anti-seizure medication right out of the bottle. After that, I bought a locked medication box. Once she realized she couldn't open the box, she would grab a butcher knife to try and pick the lock. We then had to hide all of our knives.

We were happy to see Lauren become more aware, but with increased awareness came danger. We started to hide our car keys out of fear that she would take the car in the middle of the night. Part of the problem was that Lauren was on so many neuro stimulants, sleeping was hard for her. The other part of the problem was that she had severe brain damage and simple tasks were hard. I had to keep an eye on her nonstop in order to keep her safe. It's no wonder I was so exhausted each night.

Lauren was speaking more words, but not in a conversational way. She could count up to the early twenties and say all the days of the week. Sometimes she would respond with something that made sense and other times it was gibberish. For lunch one afternoon I made her a grilled cheese. After placing it in front of her at the table, she looked disgusted and, clear as day, said, "God help me."

The whole family was dying laughing. Lauren was always a healthy eater and worked extremely hard to maintain her petite figure. She was not one of those lucky girls who were naturally thin; she had to work really hard. Lauren would have never ordered French fries at a restaurant. She would lecture us on how unhealthy we ate . . . as she stole ten fries right off our plates. She always believed if it came off someone else's plate, there were no calories. I hoped that my unhealthy cooking choices would lead Lauren to speak more words as she protested her lunch options.

Lauren's stubbornness wasn't located only at home. She was beginning to show signs of fatigue and frustration in therapy. Now that she was walking on her own, she would get irritated and walk right out of a therapy session. Some mornings I couldn't even get her in the car to go to therapy. I would literally pull her off the couch and push her toward the driveway. She was still only around one hundred pounds, but somehow she had super human strength.

I had a goal of having Lauren's feeding tube removed before Thanksgiving. Lauren's nurse manager for her insurance told me she didn't want me to be disappointed because that was a very aggressive goal. I knew I would enjoy proving her wrong. I had to encourage Lauren to eat real food. And by encourage, I mean force feed her. I put an Ensure bottle in her hand every chance I could get. When Lauren would show some interest in food, I was always really happy. But I soon learned that she was learning how to con me into believing she was actually eating. I would find food in random places around the house. Once I found an old yogurt in my Tiffany's gift bag on my dresser. Dave had bought me a necklace from Tiffany & Co. on our trip to New York that March. Nothing crazy expensive, but it was a great memento from our trip. Lauren helped me pick it out and also laid claim on it when I die. The necklace was still fine but the box and bag that it came in was full of rotten yogurt. I later found a rock hard, ham sandwich in the laundry pile; she must have thrown it down the laundry chute. Finding all this random food, I wondered if maybe I had been a little too aggressive with the feeding tube goal? Nope—Operation Force Feed was still on. Perhaps I was even *more* determined.

Lauren's therapy program was called the "Day Treatment Program." There was an hour break for lunch and all the therapists shared the same lunch hour. We really struggled during that hour. Lauren rarely ate anything they served in the cafeteria, so we relied on her tube feedings. Those feedings trickled through her feeding tube hooked to an IV pole. There was nothing to distract her during that hour, so I had resorted to hiding out in the bathroom together and making funny faces in the mirror and taking selfies. By the time her afternoon sessions started, she was already pretty much done for the day. Many times, we would be released early, because she wasn't cooperating.

My birthday was one of the most difficult and longest therapy days for me to watch. It was during our third or fourth week in the Day Treatment Program. Lauren worked on icing a cake as part of her OT therapy. She still wasn't using her right hand and I knew that she didn't really ice the cake. She wasn't capable of icing a cake at this point of her recovery. Basically she held a spatula while someone moved her arm. After the session, Lauren, along with her OT, walked out to the gym area holding the cake with candles and they started singing "Happy Birthday" to me. All of the patients in the therapy gym stopped to sing—everyone was off-key—and all I could look at was Lauren's now asymmetrical mouth the whole time she tried to sing. I know I should have been thankful for the gesture, but instead I wanted to throw the cake against the wall. This was my worst birthday in the history of birthdays. Swallowing my grief, I thanked her therapist and set the cake down with the rest of our things to bring home (and throw away) later.

During Speech that day Lauren played a Barney the Dinosaur memory game. She did okay, but I hated that they used a child's game. Couldn't they think outside the box and make one for adults, with everyday items? Her last therapy session of the day was with a therapist assistant instead of an actual therapist. The assistant tried playing the Barney memory game again and Lauren wasn't interested—most likely because she had spent the last hour playing the same stupid game. The assistant's alternative plan was saying, "Okay, instead why don't you lay your head down and rest for a while."

I was sitting in the room mortified. *This* was her therapy session? Another therapist in the room working with another patient must have seen the look on my face and intervened. She asked her to try something else instead of resting.

"Can you tell me your name?" the assistant asked Lauren.

No response.

She asked again.

Still no response.

The third time she said, "You have five minutes to tell me your name. I'll wait."

I had heard enough. "She can't tell you her name, she has aphasia," I said, fighting back my tears. "She can't understand you, and she doesn't know her name."

We sat in awkward silence for a while and when the session was over another therapist suggested I go speak with the director about Lauren's last session. I declined; I knew that I would not be able to speak without becoming a blubbery mess. I gathered my things, including the stupid birthday cake, and we headed out. I cried the whole way home; I hated that Lauren couldn't do something as simple as ice a cake or say her name. I hated brain injuries and I hated my forty-fourth birthday.

Within the first month of being home, Lauren became completely continent and learned to wash her hands and brush her teeth. Brushing her teeth became almost an obsession; she would brush her teeth ten times a day. Although we were happy she was doing these everyday tasks, we still had a few challenges. She didn't care whose toothbrush she used, and she always spit on the floor. She would also throw her toilet paper on the ground instead of the toilet, and only wash her left hand. I didn't complain, progress is progress.

In early September, construction started on our house. The crew began with the wheelchair ramp extension on the side of the deck. It was weird waking up and doing our routine with men right outside our kitchen window. I could no longer roll out of bed *as is* and pee with the bathroom door open to keep an eye on Lauren. I was extra thankful Lauren had therapy, so we had somewhere to go.

Insurance was paying for our remodel (another advantage of work comp) and offered to pay for us to be in a rental house during construction. Finding a rental house big enough for our family (including Grandma) wasn't an easy task. One problem was finding a house that would let us sign a short lease. The other obstacle was finding something close to home. I had a huge support system in my neighborhood. I couldn't ask friends who picked up our kids for soccer practice twice a week to drive an extra twenty minutes out of their way. Both Ryan and Maggie played soccer; life didn't slow down because Lauren had an accident.

We ultimately decided to stay in our house during the construction process. Looking back, I don't know if that was the best choice, but I missed being in my own home, my own bed, and more importantly my own, big bathtub.

Dave had been back at work for a while and we were trying hard to make the best of our new life. In October we celebrated Lauren's twenty-sixth birthday. In the morning, one of Lauren's friends picked her up and took her for a manicure. A birthday dinner was planned with her friends later that evening. She seemed genuinely happy and I felt extremely grateful. Six months earlier I never thought she would make it through the weekend, much less celebrate her next birthday.

During dinner Lauren thought her fingernails were still wet. The light directly over their table was bright and made her freshly manicured nails extra shiny. The girls were laughing when they told me how Lauren refused to hold her glass with her fingers. She picked everything up with her palms so she wouldn't mess up her nails. At least the girl still had her priorities straight.

Most of Ryan's freshman soccer games were scheduled at 4:00 p.m. right after school. I could have easily brought Lauren in her wheelchair to catch a game or two, as her therapy ended at 3:00 p.m. and the highway home ran alongside Ryan's high school. But I didn't. I was afraid that if we showed up, Ryan would be embarrassed of his sister in front of his new friends. Instead, I made the decision to continue to be an absent parent. I wish I had been stronger and should have asked Ryan how *he* felt, but I was trying to protect him. I still wonder if I made the right choice. This was not the kind of mother I wanted to be; I was consumed with piecing Lauren back together as best as I could.

———

Lauren was starting to display many "quirks" and obsessions at home, with hiding food in strange places just the tip of the iceberg. She would go to every closet in the house and start pulling all the clothes off the hangers, she would dig through dresser drawers as if she was desperately searching for something. It was tough to witness. I was at a loss as to how to help her. A dangerous new quirk was taking several baths a day. It felt like every time I turned around, I would find her in the bathtub with the water running. I had no idea how she could silently sneak past six other people in the house, get undressed by herself, and climb in the tub unnoticed. Her sneaky ninja skills left us all baffled.

On October 28, way ahead of schedule, Lauren had her feeding tube removed. This was a huge win knowing that I was able to beat my goal of removal before Thanksgiving and gave me a boost to set the bar even higher. Unfortunately, Lauren was becoming more and more difficult in therapy. She was eating real food again, which was good, but what was *not good* was that during therapy she would walk out, go to the employee break room, and try to steal people's lunches. This was a daily occurrence. I started packing snacks in case she got hungry, but snacks didn't help. She preferred stealing lunches. To keep her from becoming known as the lunch room bandit, I had to spend a big part of my day as a human shield standing guard in front of the employee refrigerator.

We had many excellent therapists that worked with Lauren in the day program, but there was one who wasn't a good fit. I felt like this particular therapist was at a complete loss as to what to do to motivate Lauren. Perhaps this was part of the problem with Lauren not wanting to go back every day. Week after week, Lauren would make beaded or macaroni necklaces during therapy. This was worse than the Barney memory game. The old Lauren enjoyed a fast-paced life in NYC. Was working on macaroni necklaces every week the best way to motivate her?

Ultimately, the facility recommended we take a break from therapy for a few weeks due to Lauren's increasingly stubborn, bad behavior. I was afraid that Lauren's progress would stop if we took a break. I only wanted her to get better and I didn't want to wait. Her therapists had helped her so much over the last several months. I hated to leave, but sometimes change *is* good. But I didn't see how sitting at home all day with the construction crew would be helpful, especially as Lauren's increasingly bad behavior was becoming a real problem. I didn't know how to fix it, but I knew it was up to me to *try*.

Chapter Eleven

KEEPING US ON OUR TOES

'm not sure what I was expecting when we left Chicago, but I can guarantee it wasn't some of the crazy quirks Lauren had started to pick up. Living with quirks wasn't completely foreign to me, yet this was a whole new level. Dave has always been a little *quirky*. At the start of our marriage I thought some of the odd things he did were kind of cute. Through the years his cuteness has definitely dissipated and some of his habits are enough to drive me mad.

He refuses to go to a drive-thru, preferring to go inside and watch the cashier push all the buttons. He even has a certain way he orders a meal at McDonald's to *trick* them into asking more specific questions about his order to ensure accuracy. The sad part is some of my kids are picking up his weird behavior and think it's normal.

To be fair, although I am not *quirky*, some may put me in the category of *crazy*. Looking back, I often wonder if it was such a sound decision to create so many children. Sometimes I look at them and wonder, *Which one is the craziest?* Each and every one of them brings their own special brand of crazy, crazy-quirky, crazy-cuckoo, or crazy-quirky-cuckoo to the Murphy table. To the outside world it's hard to see, but Dave and I sit back and laugh watching our two sons-in-law realize they have both gotten themselves into quite the pickle.

Murphy crazy is a special kind of crazy!

Dave has a favorite parking spot at the grocery store. If it is taken, he contemplates going to a different grocery store. Back when he was a Pepsi addict, he would go to bed with a full glass of Pepsi on his nightstand. If I took a drink, he would refill it to the rim. It had to be completely full, the two-liter bottle always on the nightstand next to his glass. He rarely even drank his Pepsi at night, but it was there like a security blanket *just in case* he needed it. He has since replaced the security of his full glass of Pepsi with a weighted blanket. Stand back ladies, he's all mine. I vaguely remember learning in religion class that some people spend their purgatory while living on earth.

———

Once Lauren was home, her improvements were substantial. But just like everything else in her recovery, improvements were often a double-edged sword. Friends would come to visit and if she saw them walking up the driveway she would crawl into her bed or go upstairs and hide in one of her siblings' beds. She struggled with facing people, she was becoming more aware and it made her sad. There was one notable exception. Her friend Courtney was back living in New York, but when she was in town Lauren was always happy to see her. They had a connection that was so deep even brain injury couldn't keep them from finding a way to connect.

Lauren's speech was still pretty random and a far cry from conversational. Once while Courtney was visiting, and Lauren looked at her friend's ears and said, "Your earrings look cheap."

I loved it when she said something that was reminiscent of the old Lauren. Courtney laughed, admitting they *were* cheap, which made it even funnier. It reminded me of that last December when I was visiting Lauren in New York. It was a really cold week and the coat I brought with me wasn't very warm. This was before Uber and Lyft were available in New York, so finding a cab in the city during bad weather was tough. While Lauren was at work, I went to Macy's and bought a new mid-thigh length, white puffy coat with a fur-lined hood. I thought it looked young and trendy and it was a bonus that I bought it in New York. I felt super cool. When I saw Courtney, she even told me how cute my coat was. I was feeling pretty proud of myself that I made the right choice. Lauren showed up last, looked at my coat, and scrunched up her nose. "That coat has a really cheap looking zipper."

I rolled my eyes and told her I didn't care, and that Courtney *loved* my new coat (she probably hated it too). The entire rest of my weekend in New York I got the zipper stuck in the fabric of my *cheap* coat at least four times—a couple of times I resorted to stepping out of it in the middle of a restaurant to make it easier to fix. I hate it when my kids are right.

Back at home, Lauren and our house were both under construction, and I was realizing that neither one was going to be a quick fix. Most of the house was getting redone, so *obviously* I couldn't keep the same furniture—no, that would have been cost-effective and resourceful, words that weren't part of my vocabulary. Now I needed to find a new comforter for Kelsey and Maggie's bed and thought it would be good for Lauren to come along to get her out of the house.

The first store on our list was JCPenney's. While we were looking at the "bed in the bag" sets against the back wall, I noticed that Lauren was no longer standing next to us. The silent ninja strikes again. I panicked for a second, but knew she couldn't have gotten too far. It was literally five seconds ago that she was standing next to me and she was still a little unsteady on her feet. I rounded the corner and found her lying comfortably in one of the display beds. I'm not going to lie, many times throughout my childhood while shopping with my mom, I often thought about pulling back the covers and climbing into those comfy looking beds myself.

I tried to get Lauren up as quickly as possible without anyone in the store noticing, but she wasn't budging. I finally yanked her up with all my might. Once upright, she started walking toward another display bed. I knew this was not going to work, so I gave Kelsey my keys and asked her to take Lauren out to the car while Maggie and I looked around for a few more minutes. Maggie and I had just started looking at the rest of the comforters when Kelsey called me from the parking lot. Apparently Lauren had taken the keys away from her because she was afraid Kelsey was trying to leave without me. I realized it would have been easier to just let Lauren nap in the display beds while we took our time browsing until security noticed and escorted us out. This was one of many shopping fails with Lauren during those first few months home.

Another new thing Lauren started doing was taking items out of my shopping cart at the grocery store and putting them back on the shelves. Sometimes she would put them immediately back in the correct spot but a little crooked, other times she would start taking things from three or four aisles over and stick them anywhere. There was really no logical explanation for which items she would deem unworthy of our purchasing, but one thing we knew for sure was that if she decided it was a no, there was no way we would be able to get the item back in our cart.

On one of these shopping sprees I left Lauren and Dave in the dairy section so I could return one of her "no" items to its proper place. When I came back, I found Dave pleading with Lauren to let him put the Kraft singles back in the cart. He kept rambling on and on about how much he likes cheese on his sandwiches. They both had a tight grip on the package of cheese. I walked directly between them, grabbed the pack of cheese, put it back on the refrigerator shelf, and let Dave know that he could still enjoy his sandwiches without cheese. Besides, he didn't need the extra calories. She was saving him from himself.

This behavior wasn't limited to the grocery store. We took several trips to Target on days where she didn't have therapy. On one visit she selected a multi-colored scarf. I thought it was hideous, but she really wanted it. Turns out she got a ton of compliments and the rest of my girls all liked it. Obviously, I know nothing. I was just a mom in a cheap coat with a broken zipper. Several of our Target trips ended abruptly, whenever Lauren would dart toward the door. Some days I had only a few items, other times I had a full cart. When Lauren decided it was time to go, nothing could stop her. I still feel bad for whichever employee found the random abandoned carts littered around their store every week. The easiest solution would be to discontinue going out in public, but I knew I needed to find a way for her to learn proper behavior and these everyday excursions were necessary parts of therapy.

Domestic tasks were also becoming part of therapy. Lauren helped unload the dishwasher. I would give her the silverware to sort and put away (the knives were still hidden). Good thing I'm not a neat freak. Lauren either never noticed the dividers in our silverware drawer or just assumed the flatware looked best in some sort of abstract design on top of the dividers. At least they were clean.

One place that Lauren liked to go for lunch was Subway. For whatever reason, Lauren always felt really comfortable while we were ordering at Subway and would try and tell the employees what she wanted on her sandwich before I had a chance to order it for her. I knew it was best to let her do it herself, but she was still only producing gibberish and it made for a pretty awkward sandwich assembly line. I would get nervous at the counter wondering what Lauren might say. Shannon was with me the day Lauren was asked by an employee what she would like on her sandwich and Lauren stood up tall and said with complete confidence and tone, "Umm, University of Lettuce."

Shannon and I immediately busted out laughing. It came out of nowhere. The poor employee just looked at us like we had all lost our minds. The more we tried to stop laughing, the more we laughed. Lauren stood there thoroughly confused and completely void of any type of facial expression, which made the situation even funnier. I know everyone else in line thought we were on drugs. Nope, we are just a little crazy, no drugs needed. We were finally able to pull ourselves together and get the heck out of there. From that day forward I drove ten miles out of my way to a different Subway every time I wanted to get her a sandwich.

Going out to eat as a family wasn't a common occurrence. Not only was it expensive, but it was hard to coordinate schedules around sports teams, college, and work in order to get everyone together at the same time. Also, Lauren would do her very own version of dine and dash, she skipped right over the dine part. she would bolt for the door before our food even arrived. We quickly learned after the accident that I needed to have strategies in place in order for Lauren to have successful outings. One of our strategies was to have more than one car. If Lauren bolted, I could take her home and Dave could stay with the rest of our family and have our meals boxed up. There is nothing I enjoyed more that eating a cold burger with a soggy bun and French fries an hour and a half after ordering. Another strategy was to seat her in the middle of the table with her back to the front door. This often helped and every once in a while, we made it to the end of a meal.

Another quirk Lauren picked up was credit cards and writing checks. She understood the concept that things cost money but was still way off. She would try and write a check wherever we went. Sometimes she signed her name correctly, other times she would sign my name. The amount was always a crazy high amount. At therapy she would leave mid-session and give the girl at the front desk a check for $3,000 for her copay. Our drywall taper got a check for $7,000.

She also went through a phase where she would take all of her credit cards and/or mine out of our wallets and carry them around stacked in her hand all day. She would not put them down to even use the bathroom (she was till only washing one hand anyway, so no need to put the credit cards down to wash her hands).

While Lauren was at RIC, Eucharistic ministers from a neighboring Catholic church would bring the patients and families Communion. Lauren was NPO, which is a Latin medical term that means "nothing by mouth." She couldn't receive Communion herself, but they brought it to me every day. I used to pray that someday Lauren would be able to take Communion again, as surprisingly church was the one place she would sit for a full hour. She was never an overly religious person, but her foundation was there, and it was rock solid. It would be hard to grow up in a big Irish Catholic family, attend twelve years of Catholic school, and not have a little bit of faith. I would love to say she went to Mass every Sunday in New York, or that all of my adult children attend Mass every Sunday, but then I would have to go to confession.

When we first started bringing Lauren to Mass with us after her accident, I would stay in the pew with her during Communion. Eventually, when she was becoming more and more aware, she got in the Communion line. I hoped memory would kick in and she would remember what to do. *This time would be different. This was special.* When she went up to receive Communion she brought with her many gifts, or rather *gift cards*, her left hand clutched a stack of at least ten Visa gift cards, Starbucks Rewards, Loft and Nordstrom credit cards—all the good ones. I'm not sure what type of a transaction she thought she would be entering into with God. (Was there a reward program?)

One morning I saw Lauren at the sink brushing her teeth (for probably the tenth time of the day). She was in our powder room, which was unusual. I went in to check on her and she looked at me and smiled. Her teeth were covered in something black. She had been brushing her teeth with a mascara wand. *Is that mascara, or maybe it's Maybelline?*

Her therapists explained this was normal and all part of the healing process. Her brain was figuring things out and mascara wands and toothbrushes are both long and thin. It was kind of ironic that the girl who kept Crest Whitestrips in business while she was in high school was now brushing her teeth with mascara.

Despite some of the craziness, I could definitely see in her eyes that things were becoming clearer and more focused. Dave always described it like he felt she was covered in a thin veil, everything just out of reach. She was so close we could see it; we just couldn't quite figure out how to remove that veil and bring our Lauren back to us. Fortunately for me, I never realized how thick that *thin* veil really was. I was still sad all of the time, through my own veil of sadness. I searched for the positive. I kept coming back to the words of Dr. Chen: *Find the positive*. Many days I had to reach further than I knew was humanely possible. But if I looked hard enough, it was there.

My days were hard and extremely long, but through all the craziness and relearning, there were bright new beginnings and Lauren was working her way back to us. This was the stage where I perfected the silent cry. I was the strong one. It was up to me to fix this, that was my job. Dave's job was to support all my crazy ideas and love me despite my constant sadness. He is the only one who truly knew how bad things really were. On Facebook and CaringBridge and Instagram, things were fabulous, but every night I went to bed and soaked my pillow with hundreds of quiet tears. I would relive the events of the day and plead with God to show me a way and give me the wisdom to make things better. We needed our Lauren back and Dave and the kids needed regular cuckoo Colleen to return.

Chapter Twelve

SO MANY FACEBOOK FRIENDS

Shortly after Christmas, Lauren began rehab at a new outpatient facility. But before they could add her to their daily schedule, we had to go in for an evaluation. Lauren insisted on wearing jeans, high-heeled boots, and her new multicolor scarf. (Fresh lipstick was a given.) As we worked with the different therapists, I looked around and realized that I should have been more convincing in regard to her outfit. Lauren stuck out like a sore thumb; she was the only patient in the gym area wearing high-heeled, over-the-knee go-go boots.

We made it through the evaluation without her trying to steal anyone's lunch (most likely because she couldn't find the break room). I decided not to mention her issues and surprise them the following Monday.

Something new that had started for Lauren was severe stomach pain. We were at a loss. We took her for a CT scan thinking it might have been her shunt wire—a wire that ran from her brain, down the side of her neck, and drained into her stomach cavity—causing issues. Lauren was thin enough where you could see the wire through her skin down the side of her neck. Doctors said she would never be able to detect that it was there, but Lauren could tell.

The CT scan came back with no abnormalities.

Lauren's pain continued. Because I felt that I was basically a doctor at this point, I thought she could be constipated. I gave her Ex-Lax pills, but they didn't help, so I gave her two more right before a nap.

Lauren hated her hospital bed. She normally slept wherever she could find a place. This was nothing new. Before she moved to New York, she moved home for a few months to save money. She made a point to go to sleep before her sisters so she could get first pick of not only beds but which side of the bed she wanted. It didn't matter that it wasn't her bed—she was older and wiser and always got there first.

On this particular day she chose Kelsey's bed to take a nap. Lauren had been completely continent at this point—*had* being the key word. It's amazing how many times in life I felt my expired cosmetology license made me so intuitive to all things medical. I was patiently waiting for gentle overnight relief when I heard the bathwater running upstairs. Lauren must be awake and ready for her fifth or sixth bath of the day. I went to check on her and was immediately hit with a rotten smell at the top of the stairs. I thought, *Oh crap.* Literally. There was crap everywhere. I followed the long trail of diarrhea to its origin in the middle of Kelsey's bed, where it then cascaded down the side of the mattress and bedframe, leading all the way to the bathroom and into the tub. When I reached Lauren in the bathtub, she looked at me in confusion. To clarify, more confused than what was typical. Poor thing, she had to be wondering, what just happened?

I kept thinking back to Dr. Chen's "look for the positive." Well, let's see, I overdosed my trusting daughter on laxatives and had about forty minutes to clean this poop up before Kelsey arrived home. If she knew Lauren pooped all over her bed, I would be back at JCPenney not only buying new bedding but a brand-new bed as well. The positive . . . I knew I could find the positive, and there it was.

I could definitely rule out constipation as the source of Lauren's stomach pain.

My next theory was something I dreaded. Maybe the pain was related to her endometriosis? I knew I would have to arrange an appointment with her obstetrician. I wished I could insert the Collen Murphy way of fixing things on this one. Back in the day, whenever I would hear a funny noise while driving my car, I would just turn up the radio because I couldn't afford a car repair. If I couldn't hear the squeaky brakes, they weren't squeaky.

If a tree falls in the forest and no one is there to hear it, does it really make a sound?

Earlier, I was talking to Sam about all of Lauren's increasing stomach pain, and she first suggested that maybe Lauren should see an obstetrician. I had already concluded that I needed to take her, but I was hoping it would fix itself like my old brakes. I also secretly hoped Sam would offer to take her. Now that she was a full-fledged adult, I could no longer make her do my dirty work.

Once when Sam and Lauren were little, I left the house without any cash. Sam had an indoor soccer game in Illinois, about a forty-minute drive from our house. This was a fairly new team and I didn't know the other moms that well. I always felt because of my young age, it was hard to get their approval and I didn't fit in. I would go far out of my way to try and prove my worth. At the girl's school, I was the Daisy Girl Scouts leader, the room mom, the candy bar chairman—you name it, I was volunteering. But these moms weren't school moms; they were soccer moms. They didn't know me yet and I felt intimidated.

On our way to the game I noticed that the gas gauge was nearly on *E*. My plan was to ask one of the other moms if she could lend me five or ten dollars for enough gas to get home. But I chickened out; I couldn't do it. And this was before cell phones or debit cards, so I had no way of calling Dave to come and rescue me. My pride got in the way of a logical solution. I didn't want to be known as not only the floozy mom who had kids too young, but now I would be the floozy, *panhandler* mom.

I had an alternate plan. I was going to search under the seats of my car and the bottom of my purse until I came up with some money to get a gallon or two of gas. When we got in the car post-game, I let the girls know we would be coasting home on fumes and a few Hail Mary prayers would be greatly appreciated. I turned the radio up, knowing from experience that it would help. Ten miles from home, I pulled into a gas station. Lauren was asleep in the backseat. I handed Sam my wad of change, and with the straightest face I could muster, I asked her to bring it inside and tell the clerk to please put thirty-seven cents on pump 3.

I will be spending the rest of my days trying to apologize for making her ask for thirty-seven cents in gas. Thankfully we made it home with our dignity intact. Well, maybe not Sam's dignity, but mine was good. Lauren later told us she was not asleep; she just wanted to ensure Sam was the one picked for the job.

Thanks to an extra-large dose of Catholic guilt, I knew I couldn't ask Sam to take Lauren to the OB. This would be my job. I called the office to ask for special accommodations, as I knew that once we signed in, we had a small window of around forty seconds before Lauren would try and find her escape route.

Sitting in a doctor's office was worse than sitting in a restaurant. Luckily, they were very accommodating. They ushered her right back to an examination room. Fortunately everything checked out okay with her IUD and that was not the source of her pain.

Many times, her pain was so intense that she would take off her pants in the car on the way home. With our garage door opener broken, it was becoming increasingly difficult trying to figure out the best way to get my pantless daughter into the house every afternoon without the neighbors or construction crew noticing. This was in the middle of January. Thankfully, she would put her shoes back on, but most days she walked inside with nothing on her bottom half other than her knee-high boots. She sure kept life interesting.

Lauren's new speech therapist quit after her evaluation, pawning her off on someone else. Something about not having enough time in her schedule. My best guess was that after she met Lauren she was like, "Holy cow, I have no clue how to help this girl."

Luckily her replacement was great. We grew to love all of our new therapists. We especially loved the front office people, and they loved Lauren. What's not to love? Every day she greeted them with a smile and a three-thousand-dollar check.

Lauren's occupational therapist found a solution to her stealing lunches. Instead of fighting the unusual behavior, she used it as part of therapy. She showed Lauren where the peanut butter was kept in the cabinet and made sure there was always fresh bread. Making a peanut butter sandwich wasn't easy for Lauren with her right-hand weakness. Continuing the food rewards approach, her speech therapist used Wheat Thins to try and bribe Lauren to cooperate. She was definitely well fed while working on her recovery.

Unfortunately Lauren's door dashing was getting out of control. I sarcastically suggested tying her to the chair with bungee cords and duct tape, but her therapists didn't feel like that was the best possible solution. Many times I was out in the parking lot wrestling with Lauren to go back inside. These were tough times.

I knew she couldn't get better without therapy and she hated everything about it (except for the peanut butter sandwiches). Anyone who works with the neuro population knows that this type of behavior can happen, especially in injuries as severe as Lauren's, but knowing it's typical doesn't make it any easier.

On one occasion I was outside holding on to Lauren as she tried to run away. She pulled away with such force, I was left holding only her coat. She was like a raging bull and headed alarmingly toward a busy intersection. I needed to get a handle on the situation immediately and get her back to safety. When she wouldn't respond to me yelling at her to stop, I smacked her across the face. She stopped and looked directly at me with shock, sadness, and anguish. Next, she crumbled into my arms and cried. I stood there in the dead of winter, hugging my broken baby girl in the middle of a parking lot next to a busy intersection with cars whizzing by, trying to process what had just happened. I looked at her expensive designer coat left behind in a crumpled heap in the middle of the parking lot as an unwelcome metaphor of her old life, she was being left behind as life continued forward without her. We didn't try to go back inside, we got in the car and tearfully headed home.

Coming home after a day like that wasn't easy; our construction crew was always there. This would be a day that I needed to spend some time in the fetal position processing what had just happened. Did I seriously smack my brain injured daughter? What was wrong with me? Couldn't I have found an alternative way to guide her back to safety? Who hits a person with brain damage? I felt like I was failing at everything. Was I doing what was best? Should I have listened to the other facility and just taken a break? Was I pushing her too hard?

Would things ever get better?

Shortly after the parking lot fiasco, a new quirk emerged totally out of left field. Lauren became obsessed with our attic; she would go down the upstairs hallway and point to the opening while showing signs of severe distress. She would go to the same spot over a dozen times a day trying to find a way up there. I never paid attention to that opening before. The only one I was aware of was in the garage where we stored our artificial Christmas tree. One day Lauren pulled several Rubbermaid storage boxes full of summer clothes into the hall, stacked them together, and tried to climb them like Spider-Man for attic access.

While the ever-present construction crew was working on the house, Lauren would watch them like a hawk. The second they would step off their ladder, she would be dragging it down the hall toward the attic. We loved our construction crew and were grateful that they were so understanding to her craziness. Every night they had to take their ladders with them so that we could keep Lauren safe.

To the left of the attic opening, against the wall, is a linen closet. Lauren broke two of the wire shelves climbing up the closet trying to get closer to the attic. Some people thought Lauren had hidden something up there before the accident, but I knew that the rafters of my attic didn't contain the Irish Crown Jewels. It was simply another strange brain impulse. She no longer pulled clothes off hangers or hid food in my underwear drawer. This too shall pass. Sam even tried to show her there was nothing up there by bringing a ladder upstairs and removing the opening to the attic. It seemed as if each new urge came with more tenacity than the last one and it was becoming increasingly more difficult to divert her attention.

By spring 2014, the attic obsession went away and was replaced with Facebook friend requests. We had restored service to Lauren's phone because she enjoyed scrolling through Facebook and Instagram. She requested so many friends that Facebook threatened to suspend her, apparently people reported her. I saw several messages on her phone from people asking, "Do I know you?"

Seriously people, can't you just hit *decline friend request*. These were probably the same people in school that enjoyed their turn as the hall monitor. She also joined many Facebook support groups. She is still a proud member of over one hundred groups. Some of my favorites include: *people recovering from total knee replacements, mama space, mission trip to Mexico, I love candle giveaways, modern digital photographers,* and *I grew up in or around Spanish Lake.* Obviously, Facebook groups are considerably more inclusive than the average person.

Dave and I were invited, along with several of our other church friends, to a friend's lake house a couple of hours away. Our group spent many years together at kids' soccer games and school functions. These are my people and I was excited that the kids had offered to step up and keep an eye on Lauren so Dave and I could get away for a bit of fun.

That weekend, Sam planned a sibling night for Friday at her house. I knew Lauren would do better at home but didn't want to overstep. Sam was an adult and I didn't want to treat her like a baby. Late Saturday morning while I was at the lake, I received a phone call from Sam. I could tell right away from her shaky voice that something was wrong. "Mom, first I want to tell you that Lauren is okay," she said.

Before she could continue, she was crying. My first thought was that Lauren had a seizure. The kids had unfortunately witnessed a couple of them, and they knew what to do. But as Sam continued speaking, my head tried to process the series of events that had transpired that morning.

"Shannon woke up around 7:00 a.m. because she had to return Grandma's car," Sam said. "She walked past the room that Lauren had been sleeping in with Kelsey and Lauren wasn't there." She looked at the front door and could see sunlight coming through a small crack. Shannon started frantically searching the house, but Lauren was gone. Shannon then woke up everyone in the house. They all started running in opposite directions, searching for Lauren. Erin jumped in her car and drove to the nearest hospital. She pulled in front of the entrance, ran past the security guard, and hollered inside the ER lobby, "Do you have any Jane Does?"

They told her they did not, and she needed to move her car.

In the meantime, Sam called the police. Kelsey and Maggie stayed at the house in case Lauren came back. Sam ran through her neighborhood, peering down every driveway and alley that she passed. Erin and Kelsey had both been repeatedly calling Lauren's phone, hoping that she would pick up. Lauren eventually answered Erin's call. Erin said to her, "Lauren, find someone that looks nice and give them your phone."

Erin later told me that because of her obsession with the TV show *Criminal Minds*, she fully expected a scrambled voice to say, ""I have your sister; you have three minutes before I start cutting off her fingers."

Instead, a city cab driver got on the phone and was thoroughly confused. Erin told him where to bring Lauren and then hung up. Two seconds later, she called Lauren back and had her stay on the phone until she arrived safely in front of Sam's house.

The cab driver pulled up to a police car in front of the house and several hysterically crying Murphy girls. Lauren got out of the cab and told Erin, "I was so scared." Sam's husband, John, paid the cab driver. Her cab fare was well over a hundred dollars. We now affectionately refer to the fare as Lauren's *ransom money*. The kids were so excited to see Lauren back home safe and sound that they didn't think to ask specifics—where he picked her up, what she was saying, where she asked him to take her? All we know is that she tried to write him a check. Unfortunately, she used her checkbook with her New York address.

In this stage of her recovery, Lauren was still unable to communicate her name or address or phone number. When Lauren went missing, she was still in her pajamas and wearing flip-flops. Thankfully, she brought her purse and phone with her. Sometime that morning, Lauren bought a fountain soda from a gas station. Later, Sam, a.k.a. Nancy Drew, took the paper cup with her to area gas stations until she matched where it came from. The cup was from a gas station on the corner of a very busy road. We can only assume Lauren bought (or stole) the soda and then hailed the cab.

Over the phone, I calmly told Sam it would be okay. No one was hurt and sometimes things just happen. I really wanted to say, "Are you all a bunch of idiots?" Which genius child of mine decided to put Lauren in bed with the kid who could sleep through a jackhammer at a rock concert located next door to an air force base?

After hanging up, I went to find Dave out on the dock and told him what happened.

His first inclination was that we should pack up and head home. I told him that we should stay. I didn't want the kids to think we thought they were incompetent. His response? "Clearly they are completely incompetent."

Point taken, but we decided to stay at the lake. What was done was done. It took me several hours to process what had happened and how dangerous it could have been. Dave spent the rest of the day/evening in a state of shock. I took the alcoholic approach. I rarely drink; I am like a unicorn among Irish Catholics. Today would be different. I felt that if ever there was a day to rethink my non-drinking lifestyle, this was it.

On Monday at therapy, I explained what had happened to Lauren's speech therapist. She got right to work teaching Lauren how to put in emergency contact information into her phone and how to find it. I also contacted an alarm company to get an alarm system for our house. Lauren's inability to tell someone her name made us fearful of a repeat disappearance.

Lauren's speech disorder was called aphasia. They mentioned it back at RIC, but we were too busy dealing with other issues like diapers, feeding tubes, C-Diff, and seizures to fully understand how much aphasia was going to affect her recovery. Aphasia kept her from understanding what we said to her. How can you gauge someone's cognitive ability when they can't understand the question? Imagine having to take your ACT or SAT test for college in Chinese. Your intelligence is gauged on how you answer the specific questions and you have no idea what the words even mean. I had no real way of knowing what Lauren was thinking or understanding. In my heart I had to believe she was capable of regaining much more of her language skills. For a long time I lived in denial. I felt like she understood me, but most of the time she didn't. She was becoming excellent at faking her way through. I googled the word aphasia so many times, I think those letters have rubbed off my computer's keyboard. I could not find a source anywhere that indicated there was a cure for aphasia. On the flip side, I couldn't find a source that said there was *not* a cure. I had to find a way to help her.

Once Lauren began making it through a full session of therapy, I started looking for our next move. I had to keep pushing, I spent many sleepless nights searching for answers. I was determined to find the right people to help piece Lauren back together. I stumbled upon an intensive speech therapy program in Florida, but one of the requirements was that the patient needed to be able to endure five hours of therapy each day. I decided if I could consistently get her to complete her regularly scheduled three hours of therapy, I would lie on the application and tell them she would be fine with five. I put in a request with our insurance adjuster, and after several weeks, the approval came through.

We were scheduled to go to Florida at the end of August through the beginning of October. The timing was perfect. Sam and John were getting married in

November. I was hopeful that Lauren's speech would improve enough that she could have real conversations with friends and family at the wedding. I knew there was no such thing as a quick fix, but I was very hopeful that the Aphasia Center would give me the tools to get Lauren that much closer to recovery.

PHOTO COLLECTION

Colleen and Lauren in 1988

Colleen and Lauren at Colleen's 40th birthday party

Lauren and Colleen at Rockefeller Center in 2012. Colleen is wearing the infamous coat with the cheap zipper.

Sam, Colleen, and Lauren having dinner in Manhattan in Dec 2012

Colleen and her girls at a family wedding, two weeks before Lauren's accident

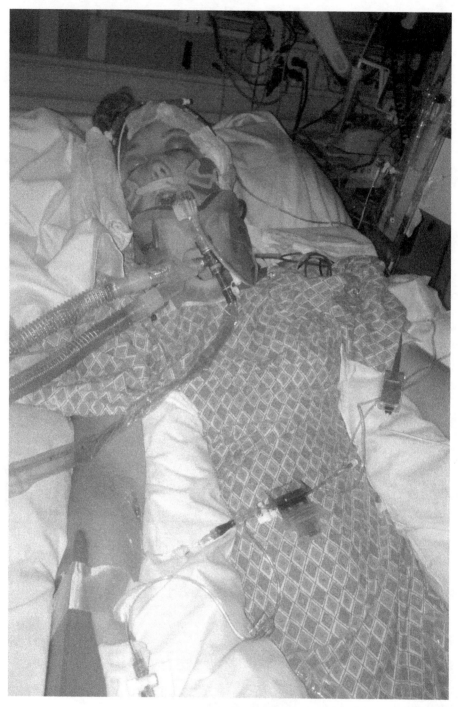

April 20, 2013, one day after Lauren's accident

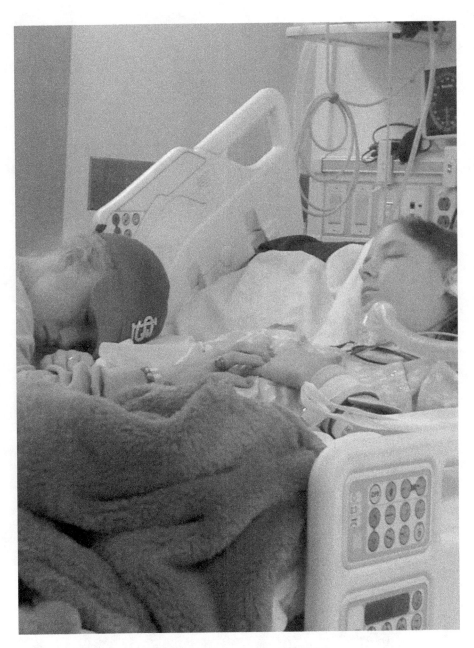

Lauren's sister, Kelsey, at Lauren's ICU bedside

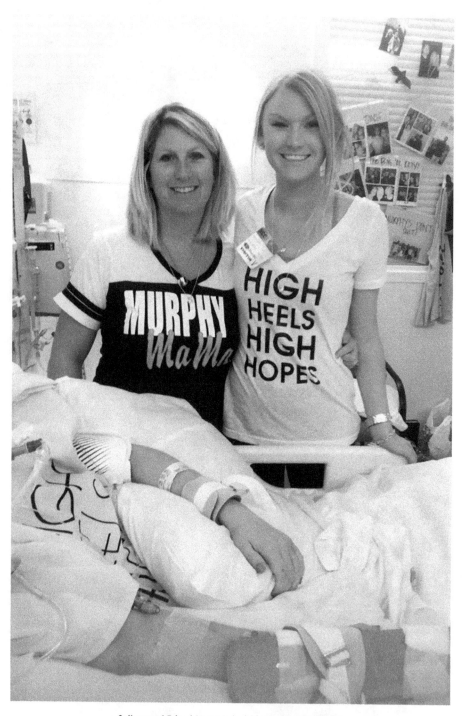

Colleen and Erin at Lauren's bedside, Mother's Day 2013

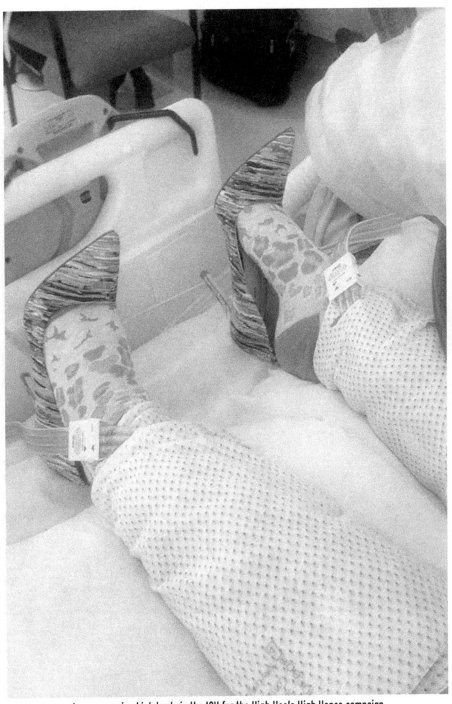

Lauren wearing high heels in the ICU for the High Heels High Hopes campaign
started by her Incarnate Word Academy Class of 2006 classmates

Dave, Colleen, and Taylor Swift in Lauren's ICU room

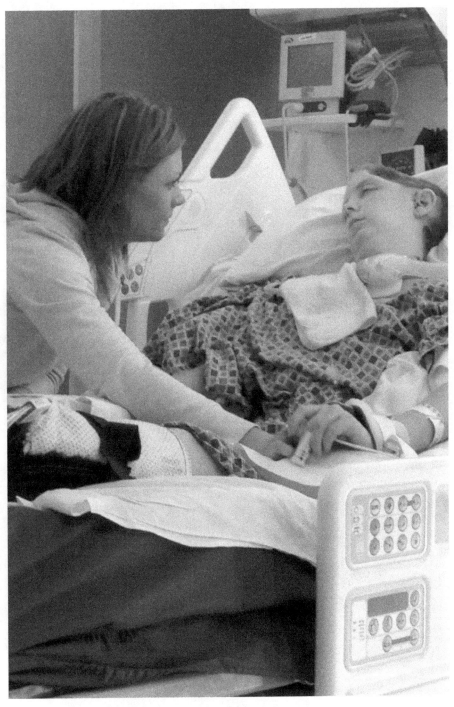

Courtney at Lauren's bedside when Lauren's head was sunken in

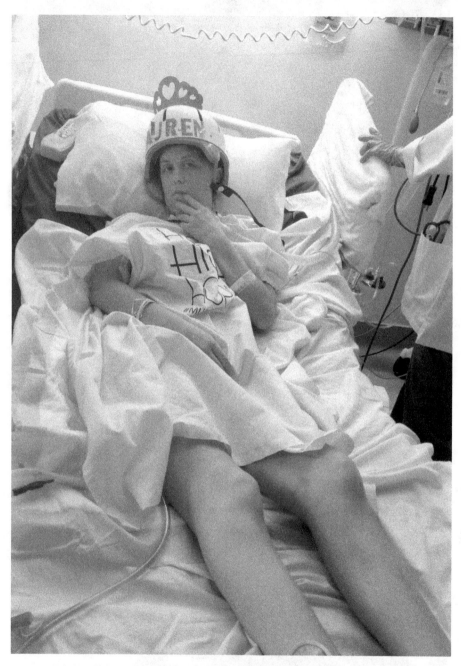

Late May 2013, wearing her custom helmet and High Heels for High Hopes hospital gown

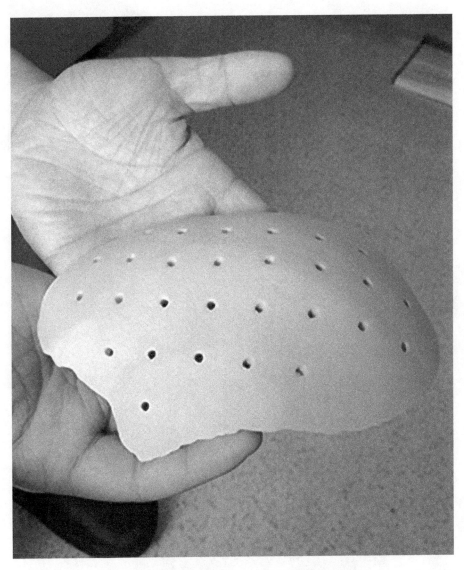

Lauren's neurosurgeon holding her prosthetic skull before surgery

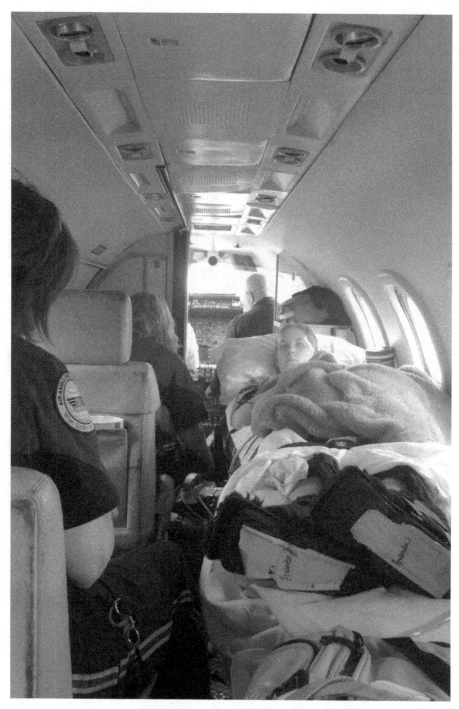

In route to Chicago in the private medical jet

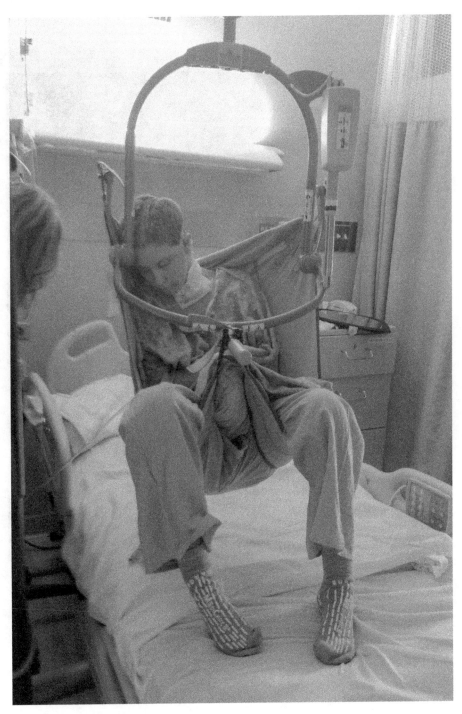

Lauren being transferred with the help of a sling on her second day at RIC

Lauren with her sister, Erin, at RIC. Her right arm was stuck in that position for several months.

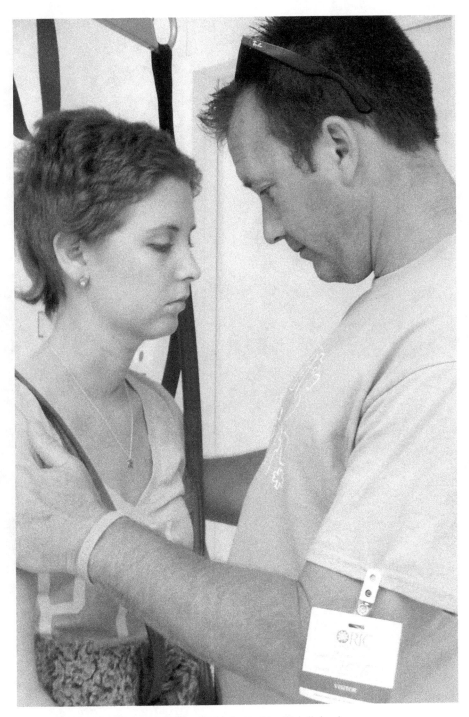

Getting a pep talk from Dad before walking the halls in a harness

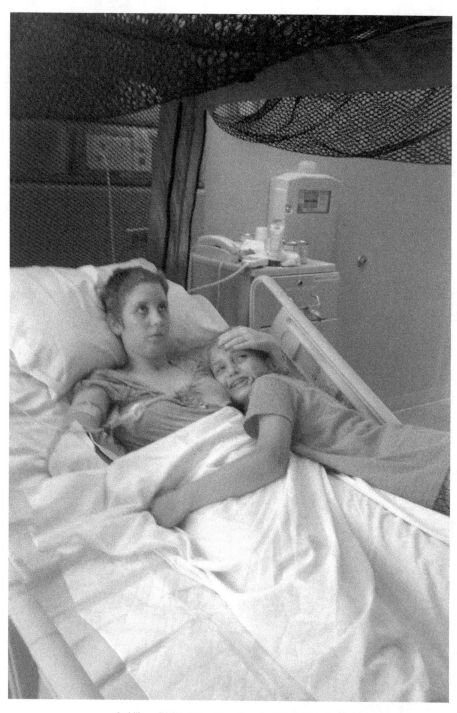

Cuddling with her little sister, Maggie, in her zip-up bed

Over 200 people welcomed us home

First night home snuggles with her siblings

Meeting Rick Springfield after a show, May 2015

Meeting Taylor Swift Backstage, September 2015

Speaking on an Aphasia Panel with members of her aphasia group, 2018

Colleen and Lauren delivering the Fontbonne University Commencement address, May 2019

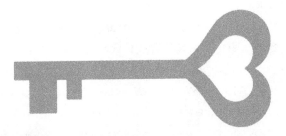

Key 3: Kindness is Free

We all know how important random acts of kindness can be; yet, for some reason, they aren't always part of our daily routines. During Lauren's recovery, my family received countless acts of kindness. One of my favorites was from a woman named April (she had kids at the same school as mine). She called the school office and put money on Ryan and Maggie's lunch cards. She covered their lunches for the rest of the school year. April thought outside the box, found a need (without being asked), and filled it with pure kindness. I didn't find out about this until months later—whether or not my kids had lunch money wasn't even on my radar.

While I was in Chicago, I came home to my apartment after a long day at RIC and found a big box on my doorstep. It was from a friend of a friend named Charlotte. She wrote me a beautiful note and explained how she prayed for our family daily. She wanted to do something special for us and decided to shop for a gift for each one of my children. She had bought each of them a special gift based on their ages and sizes. She enlisted the help of her young adult daughter and shopped at all of the trendy stores. She wanted to make sure that when my kids came to Chicago to visit, I had a special gift on hand for each one of them. I was blown away! This woman, whom I had never met, put herself in my shoes. She knew I didn't want or need anything for myself. Without even knowing me, she knew I would much rather have something to give my children. Wow, that was a powerful package!

One common mistake most of us make in an effort to be kind is to say: "Let me know if you need anything." Let's be real. For those of us (myself included) who have ever uttered those words, have you ever heard back from that person? Of course *not*. People don't typically ask for help. This is where kindness, cheerleading, and showing up all tie together. How can we be more like April or Charlotte? Don't wait to be asked; in the words of Nike, *Just Do It!*

Chapter Thirteen

THE SUNSHINE STATE

The day we left for Florida, I took a picture of Lauren at the airport standing in the exact same spot that I stood talking to Nurse John the day our lives were turned upside down. I was hopeful that Florida would be a new beginning for her. We were now sixteen months post-accident; I was desperate to find something to help speed up the slow recovery process.

Dave accompanied us to Florida to help us get settled. Lauren was difficult to handle and traveling brought a whole new layer of difficulty. Things like making sure she doesn't open the car door while I'm driving were still very much a threat.

The Aphasia Center fees included a furnished apartment in a little town called Gulfport, just outside of St. Petersburg. Dave, Lauren and I arrived in Florida on a Saturday; Dave was flying home the next day. Before we explored the area, we unpacked and stocked the apartment with groceries. Dave was very patient with me as I struggled with making decisions; I had never been so indecisive. Earlier in the day, I looked at four or five different rental cars before I finally picked one, then we went to two different grocery stores and walked inside three restaurants before I could decide on a lunch spot. This is one of the many reasons why I love him so much; he is extremely patient with my craziness. If the situation was reversed, I would have lost it back at the rental car place.

The next afternoon I dropped Dave back at the airport, and thought, *Now what?*

This was the first time Lauren and I would be alone for an extended period of time; I knew I needed to remain a step ahead of her and come up with more strategies to keep her safe. I came to Florida armed with a state-of-the-art, adhesive-backed alarm system for the front door that I bought from Amazon—not exactly a Fort Knox security system but it was better than nothing. I feared she would figure out she could just pull it off, or escape while I was in the shower. There were so many worst-case scenarios, I knew I had to sleep with one eye open.

On Monday we woke up early so I could do Lauren's hair and makeup. Afterward, we took a "first day of school" picture in front of a palm tree. Back at home, I was missing Kelsey, Ryan, and Maggie's first day of school for the second year in a row.

We arrived at the Aphasia Center on time. One of us was nervous, the other was oblivious. The Aphasia Center was in a small strip mall and set up like a doctor's office. We were given a quick tour. Each speech room had windows and a table with pads of paper, note cards, pencils, and pens. While Lauren was being introduced to her new therapists, I went back to speak with the director. I had a good feeling right away; everyone was energetic and helpful. I knew Lauren would relate well with her therapists; they were all close to her age.

This would be the first day that I would not be joining Lauren during a therapy session. I decided I should probably mention the *very slight* possibility that Lauren might try and escape. They had no way of knowing she had sneaky, silent ninja skills and superhuman strength. I considered letting them figure it out on their own but didn't want Lauren wandering around Florida or riding around in a cab.

I had paid enough ransom money/cab fare.

The director assured me that they could handle Lauren. Still, pulling out of the parking lot without Lauren I had a weird feeling, I went back to the quiet apartment and laid in the fetal position, praying they wouldn't lose her. On the positive side, I was able to pee with the door closed for the first time in ages. With the exception of the infamous lake weekend, I hadn't had that much freedom since we arrived home from RIC over a year earlier. I had no idea what to do with myself.

Five hours later, I was back at the Aphasia Center. Lauren was sitting in the lobby with one of her therapists waiting for me. They told me Lauren tried to walk out mid-morning, but they blocked the door. They set the precedent on day one that she wasn't leaving. Instead of leaving, they allowed Lauren to take frequent breaks and rest when she was feeling overwhelmed. I was happy we had chosen a place that seemed to know how to handle her difficult tendencies (probably better than I did).

That evening we went out to dinner to celebrate her first full day. I was hoping she didn't order and dash, as I had no one with me to grab our food and pay. Lauren made it through the whole dinner, but the silence was absolutely deafening. I had been living in denial in an alternate reality for so long, I didn't notice until it was just the two of us how bad things really were. Without other family members to keep the flow of conversation going, I could finally see with crystal clear clarity how severe her language deficits really were. I felt like I was back in the ICU room at Cedars trying to come up with one-sided chitchat. Lauren couldn't tell me about her day; she was a prisoner in her own mind. She could answer simple questions like "How was your day?" But she was only capable of a one-word response, which was probably not even true.

"Good."

Was it *really* good? Rumor has it you tried to escape.

We muddled through dinner and headed back to the apartment for more awkward silence. These quiet times were the absolute worst. I didn't have the distraction of the chaos at home, I was alone with my thoughts and, more importantly, my fears. I always kept a brave face and believed that she would get better. Or, did I? Was I actually fooling myself into thinking I believed that? Here we were, almost a year and a half later, and half the time she called me either "Grandma" or "Jason." I am way too young to be her grandma. Heck, I was a teenage mom. I'm technically way too young to be her mother.

And who is Jason?

Eventually my pity party dissipated, and I was back to being optimistic. Lauren was learning to write for the first time. She had been writing her name in therapy at home but had never used writing as an alternative to finding her words verbally. I was amazed to see that she was able to write the first couple of letters of a word when prompted with a photo or beginning sound. *Lipstick* was one of the first words she was able to write. Go figure.

The therapists taught not only Lauren, but also me, so much while we were there. One example is how I talk to her. If I were to ask Lauren to hand me the remote control, I might end up with a set of car keys, an apple, a tampon, or a stick of butter—none of which were even close. My old strategy would be to simply repeat the word *remote* over and over again. The Center taught me to instead say things like, "It is black, it's shaped like a rectangle, it has buttons, you use it to turn on the TV or change the volume or channel."

So simple, yet it never occurred to me. Even with this new strategy, we still struggled, but every once in a while, something clicked. It was amazing to see her excitement when she knew she got it right.

Lauren was assigned homework every night. When we finished, she would ask to go over it again. This was the first time I could see her trying to improve without my not so gentle pushing and prodding. Although we couldn't communicate like before, we could still laugh together as well as argue. Things were tough but we were tougher. Nothing is greater than a mother's love, not even aphasia. Sometimes love heals!

Meanwhile Dave was back at home doing his best muddling through his Mr. Mom duties. This would be the first year he was in charge of school supply shopping (and last). I was never the RoseArt crayons kind of mom. My kids were already burdened with a father who fell somewhere along the spectrum (we like to refer to it as *quirky*), and a mother who is, although funny, not always socially appropriate. I didn't feel that sending them to school with cheap crayons would do much for their social standing. Dave called me after this year's school supply Target run and said, "I think the kids might have taken advantage of me."

After he told me his grand total, I was confused. How could he have possibly spent that much on notebooks and folders? Well, Maggie's *pencil case* alone was seventeen dollars. She didn't see any that she liked, so one of her greedy big sisters suggested she go look in the makeup section and use a cute makeup bag instead. I wished Lauren could have been there; she would have put half that stuff back on the shelf. Dave might as well have laid down in the middle of Target as each one of our kids repeatedly drove the overflowing cart over him. I didn't even bother asking if he bought the right crayons. One can only assume they each got the sixty-four pack with the built-in sharpener.

On the weekends, Lauren and I often went to the beach. Lauren couldn't sit for hours relaxing in a beach chair anymore, so I had to get creative if I wanted her to stay for an hour or two. I always brought her iPad. We would sometimes share earbuds listening to music and singing along. She had several playlists that she would listen to when she ran in New York; I hoped the music would help her remember her old life.

Lauren was not a fan of the birds on the beach. If they got too close, she would jump up and start chasing them away—many times taking the iPad still connected to her earbuds with her. She hated the birds and I hated the spectacle she made of us every time she ran down the beach dragging an iPad muttering incoherently.

Another strategy I used to keep Lauren occupied was water aerobics. I needed something to keep Lauren's attention, conversation wasn't an option, and I was trying to lose weight for Sam's wedding. If aggressively chasing birds didn't draw enough attention to us, running in place, arm curls, and jumping jacks in the water made it more than evident that one of us was a little off, and they probably couldn't figure out which one.

At the halfway point of Lauren's program, Shannon came to Florida for a visit. As a fair-skinned redhead, the beach isn't her favorite place to go, yet I convinced her to come with us. She wasn't interested in joining our ocean aerobics class, mainly because she is terrified of sharks and equally as terrified of fish. The ocean is far from her happy place.

In the past, I literally baked Shannon on family vacations, no matter how many times we reapplied sunscreen. She always ended up spending the majority of our family vacations swimming in oversized t-shirts. Dave always teases her by saying he has seen milk darker than her.

Another reason why all my kids will need therapy.

Somehow, I talked Shannon into getting in the ocean for a minute to cool off. I was tired of listening to her complain about how hot and miserable she was. I promised her that if she got in, I would save her from the sharks. A few seconds later, we were hit by a pretty good-sized wave, and Shannon started screaming like she had just encountered a frenzy of mad sharks. According to her, a huge black fish was swimming around her ankles. She was petrified.

That officially ended our day at the beach.

When we got in the car, I asked Shannon where she put Lauren's sunglasses that she borrowed. She remembered that she had them on right before the wave hit us and the big black fish attacked her. We both realized at the same time, that "big black fish" was named Ray and his last name was Ban. Lucky for Shannon, Lauren had a head injury and had already forgotten that she lent her the expensive sunglasses. We spent the rest of the weekend hanging out and enjoying our short time together before she flew home and headed back to school.

By the end of the six-week program, Lauren's stamina had thankfully improved. I was proud of how hard she worked and watched as her growing confidence helped her to become more verbal. There was no quick fix, I knew that going in, but I still secretly hoped this six-week program would give me more of my daughter back. What it did give me were more tools to help her fight for her words.

Back at home, her regular speech therapist was receptive to taking some of the things Lauren did at the Aphasia Center and incorporating them into her daily sessions. I vowed early on that I would go to the ends of the earth to find the best therapists, and so far, so good.

A week after we returned from Florida, we traveled to Indiana for my niece's wedding. Lauren had been awake since early that morning without a nap. I was impressed that she made it through the wedding and stayed until the end of the reception. Her stamina was slowly improving. She had replaced door dashes with the "Irish goodbye." When Lauren went for her purse, we knew we were immediately out the door, no time for goodbyes.

The morning after the wedding, we woke up in the hotel and headed right over to my nephew's house for breakfast. It was Lauren's twenty-seventh birthday. As soon as we walked into the house, Lauren started turning around in circles like a dog chasing its tail. I was the only one who noticed something wasn't right. I grabbed her by her shoulders and saw the dreaded eye blinks. I called out for help and everyone kind of froze. And by froze I mean literally froze. I looked over and said, "Can someone call 911."

I not so gently said it again. "Someone, PLEASE call 911!"

The seizure lasted three or four minutes. During seizures all I can do is try and hold Lauren's head, stroke her hair, and pray for the seizure to end quickly. Looking around the room I could see fear and panic on all the faces of my loved ones: my kids, my future sons-in-law, my nephew, his wife, and Dave. There was nothing easy about any of this. We could hear the ambulance in the distance as Lauren's seizure was ending. What would we do without our first responders? The paramedics checked her vitals. We decided against taking her to the hospital. We knew from experience they would draw blood, make us wait three hours for the results, and tell us to follow up with her neurologist at home. I felt it was best for us to get her home as quickly as possible.

We had a four-hour car ride ahead of us.

The night before, I had been proud of her for not napping. What the heck was wrong with me? I should have known better. Her body couldn't be pushed so hard. Being tired made her susceptible to danger. It was up to *me* to keep her safe. I should have made sure she was able to take a nap. I felt like I had failed yet again.

Happy Birthday, Lauren. Next year I'll be better, I promise.

———

Lauren's door dashing wasn't entirely in the past. During a visit to the doctor she got frustrated and decided she would be leaving five minutes after we arrived. I had already discussed her impulsivity in regard to leaving with her doctor; at least now he could see I wasn't exaggerating. He looked at me and said, "Let her go. We can continue her appointment while we walk."

This little display gave him a window into what made Lauren Murphy tick. We followed her around as she walked back and forth, as she frantically searched for an escape route. She eventually found her way to the elevator. After witnessing this firsthand, her doctor suggested we look for a behavior therapist. I spent the next week searching, not just any behavior therapist-we needed one that specialized in traumatic brain injury and one that had superpowers and could help a girl who couldn't understand anything you said to her. I thought to myself, *This should be easy.*

I must have talked to thirty people. Finally, I found one place that had experience with traumatic brain injuries. I figured I wouldn't jinx it by mentioning her aphasia. The receptionist asked if we had insurance. When I told her that yes, Lauren was insured, she said, "I'm sorry, we only work with patient's that are uninsured."

I was really confused. That was their policy, no exceptions. I asked her if I could call back and we could start this conversation over. "Hello, my name is Colleen, my daughter has some behavior issues and to top it all off, we don't have health insurance."

She didn't find me amusing and let me know that's not how it works. I hung up the phone and realized I needed a drink, and by this time I also needed to find a behavior therapist for me too.

Lauren was on several medications: a few neuro stimulants, anti-seizure medications, and an antidepressant. She had put on quite a bit of weight that summer and we feared it could have been caused by one of her medications. I knew it bothered her, but I wasn't willing to risk her safety by switching medications. Lauren has always been vain; she was sad about her weight gain. Even though she wasn't able to verbalize her frustrations, she was able to get her point across by gesturing. One day Lauren got out of the shower, stood in front of her full-length mirror and said, "There's fat f**k Lauren."

Verbal progress is progress, even if it's The F Word. I thought it was hilarious; she did not.

Lauren's first visit back to New York was scheduled for a couple of weeks after her Indiana seizure. Resting in NYC is nearly impossible. A large group of my girlfriends were going to see *Beautiful: The Carole King Musical* on Broadway. Lauren would be staying at Courtney's new apartment. Before our trip, I talked to Lauren about where we were going. I didn't know how much she actually understood. The night before we left, I ran to Walgreens to get Lauren's prescriptions filled. When I came home, Lauren was wearing a NYC sweatshirt. She understood. It was her way of showing me she knew where we were going. I was thankful for these little moments. In my heart I believed that she was aware, but it was nice to receive concrete confirmation every once in a while.

I was hoping our trip back to the city would somehow jar her memory. She enjoyed her time visiting with Courtney, but New York didn't seem to be remotely familiar to her. Once again, I felt like I was pushing her too hard. I had imagined some type of dramatic moment of her remembering her life in New York, possibly skipping down 42nd Street while singing "Empire State of Mind" by Jay-Z. That moment never came.

Our New York trip was in mid-October and Sam's wedding was a little less than a month away. I knew that I needed to come up with a plan for Lauren to have a successful day. Courtney was flying in to help; she would be Lauren's shadow for the day and take her back to the hotel for a nap before the reception. Even with Courtney there to help, most of my focus that day was on making sure Lauren was okay. Unfortunately, brain injury doesn't take days off, even if one of your other daughter's is getting married.

The morning of the wedding, the bridesmaids (all twelve of them) were meeting at Sam's house for hair and makeup. I decided to stay home and have Lauren's and my hair done at our quiet house. I was sad that I couldn't be part of the festivities at Sam's, but I knew Lauren had to be well rested. A seizure would have ruined everyone's day.

Years ago, when I envisioned my daughter's wedding day, I never pictured myself sitting alone in a quiet house waiting for my adult daughter to finish a nap.

Sam's wedding was beautiful, and Lauren made it through the day seizure-free. Every day I felt as if I was engaged in a constant battle within myself. I was incredibly thankful that Lauren survived the accident, yet at the same time I was incredibly sad. I grieved someone who was standing directly in front of me. I missed the old Lauren, the Lauren who would be brutally honest when she didn't like my outfit or my hairstyle or my shoes (my shoes were always all wrong). I missed her laugh and her terrible singing in the car and how she always acted like she was a big help before family parties when in actuality, all she ever did was clean the glass coffee table. I missed it all—the good, the bad, and the ugly. I missed my Lauren so much it hurt. I have read that this is called *ambiguous grief*. That's a pretty big word. Not gonna lie, I had to look up the definition. In a nutshell it means that I am grieving the loss of my daughter yet feeling like a total bonehead because of the guilt because she is still here with me. I have a few friends that have lost children. I know they would give anything to be in my ugly shoes and that is what helps keep me moving forward every single day.

Chapter Fourteen

FIONA

I am pretty fortunate because Dave is the type of guy that rarely yells or gets mad. On the few occasions when he does, it's normally at the end of the day. The older he gets, the slightly more impatient he gets. Several years ago, the kids started calling him Fiona (from the movie *Shrek*). Clearly, they are terrified of him since they call him Fiona to his face.

Lauren's injury was really hard on Dave. He slowly became a quiet, moody, withdrawn version of Fiona. Men are fixers. If something is broken, they fix it. Dave was no exception. He could fix anything. He even created a special tool to unclog our bathtub drains from the many clumps of hair from the Murphy girls. He loved his role of being the fixer, especially for his girls. He was a master at making extra holes on belts or shoe buckles, always their knight in shining armor. Lauren was the exception—she couldn't be fixed, at least not quickly.

January of 2015, he became so quiet and withdrawn I was beginning to lose patience. There was no getting through to him. I thought, *If this nit-wit thinks I'm sticking around while he acts like a big baby, he's got another thing coming.*

My job with Lauren was emotionally draining. I couldn't do it alone. I needed his help; he couldn't just hide in our room to be alone when things get tough.

I left a job that I loved when Lauren had her accident. I don't regret my decision for a second. Lauren needed me. It had been almost two years since I left my career behind. I didn't have a college degree. My résumé had enough holes it could be Swiss cheese. I had to think long term and I thought about going back to school to get my degree. I always hated that I didn't have an education. I dropped out of high school at seventeen when I was pregnant with Lauren. When I met Dave, he was a single dad raising Sam. We never felt like a blended family because we weren't. The girls were two and three when we got married. In our eyes, Sam was mine and Lauren was Dave's, plain and simple.

I loved my husband, but I didn't know how to help him through this, nor did I have the energy. If things didn't begin to change, I felt there was no way I was going to spend the rest of my life with this sad sack. I may have dozed off for a bit when the priest said, "Do you take this man for better or worse?"

In hindsight, I'm sure living with me at that time was also a real treat, but Dave was too good and loyal to consider bailing, unlike me.

———

By February, Fiona was back in her cave and I was registered for school. Even though I no longer wanted to kill Dave in his sleep I felt college would still be a healthy outlet for me. Honestly, I think I really needed a break from the daily demands of trying to *fix* Lauren.

On my first day of class, I was nervous. I was afraid to arrive too early because I feared my classmates would think I was the teacher. I assumed there wouldn't be too many forty-five-year-old undergrads. When class was over, I drove two hours to Kelsey's college sorority Mom's Weekend. Like everything else in the last few years, I could never be fully present for my other children. I only stayed for one night because Dave, Lauren, and I were flying to Chicago the next day for a medical evaluation at RIC.

Lauren's insurance company had requested the evaluation since we were approaching the two-year anniversary of her accident. There is a term they use in the insurance world called MMI (maximum medical improvement). Once a doctor declares Lauren has reached MMI, her insurance may attempt to stop paying for therapy and settle her case. They had been very generous with Lauren's treatments thus far and I didn't want anything to change. Knowing the potential impact if declared MMI, I was really nervous about these tests but needed to focus on Kelsey first, one day at a time.

While I was with Kelsey at Mom's Weekend, Dave had strict instructions to take Lauren to get her nails done. I also arranged for Lauren's friend Diane to come over Sunday morning to straighten Lauren's hair. Once again, I was worried about all the "important" things for Lauren's evaluation. When I arrived home Sunday, we had only an hour to spare before leaving for the airport. Dave had followed instructions but let Lauren pick out her own nail color at the salon. She went with hooker neon pink. Obviously, I had to repaint them.

On the plane to Chicago, a baby was crying. Lauren really struggles with loud noises. Every time the cries would get louder, Lauren would groan. I explained to her that an airplane is a scary place for a baby. The baby's little ears were probably popping because of the altitude and maybe she was in pain. Lauren sat there and thought about it for a minute. I figured I really got through to her until she leaned over and whispered in my ear, "I hate that fu**ing baby."

Thank God she whispered it. Why is it that she always has the best sentences when it's highly inappropriate and involves The F Word?

———

It was surreal being back at RIC. Lauren and I were both in a much better place than our last visit. I was proud to see her walk down the same halls that she previously needed a harness to simply hold her up. It was nice to see Dr. Ballard, who was thrilled with Lauren's amazing progress. Best of all, he did not feel that Lauren had reached MMI. Lauren would continue to move forward toward recovery, which I wholeheartedly agreed. But then Dr. Ballard suggested we look into sending Lauren to a transitional living facility to teach her how to live more independently. My initial reaction to that suggestion was "Over my dead body."

Dave and I were in total agreement. We told Sam and Erin the ridiculous thing that Dr. Ballard suggested, and they looked at us like *we* were the crazy ones. They believed it could be helpful for Lauren to gain a little independence. I was forced to take a step backward and question who I was trying to protect.

What was best for *Lauren*? Did it really matter who helped Lauren the most? Was I being selfish by not wanting to give up the reins? I called QLI to schedule a visit—the same facility in Omaha, Nebraska that came to talk to me two years earlier when Lauren was still an inpatient at RIC.

Kelsey came home for summer break in time to join Lauren and me on our visit to QLI. Kelsey loves to sleep; she can fall asleep anywhere. As a result of her frequent naps, she has bed head almost every day. When we arrived at QLI, the admission director walked over to Kelsey, stuck out her hand and said, "You must be Lauren, nice to meet you."

Lauren's hair and makeup were on point thanks to her personal stylist (me), but Kelsey was another story.

Our first impression of QLI was good. Making me laugh is always a positive. I was really impressed with everything I saw and, more importantly, Lauren seemed to like it. She was finally at a stage in her recovery that she could understand why we were there. I came prepared and had a full page of typed out questions. I secretly hoped there would be a valid reason why this place wasn't a good idea, but there wasn't. The residents seemed happy and well cared for and the staff were loving and compassionate people.

I had a big decision to make. Obviously, I would discuss it with Dave, but I knew he would leave it up to me to make the final decision. Lauren's insurance company encouraged QLI based on Dr. Ballard's recommendation. It was not lost on me that many of our fellow brain injury families didn't have an insurance company that was so generous; they had to fight their insurance companies for every single therapy session. My biggest hesitation was that I wouldn't be able to stay on campus with Lauren. I understood she couldn't learn independence if I was sleeping in the bed next to her, but I wasn't willing to drop her off in Omaha and head home. Our insurance company agreed to let me go with Lauren to Omaha and pay for a furnished apartment and a rental car. They also agreed to allow Lauren to go back to the Aphasia Center in Florida for another six-week session before being admitted to QLI.

The last time Lauren finished the program at the Aphasia Center we saw a drastic improvement in her speech. Her neurologist even noticed the progress at her next appointment; he felt it was like someone turned on a light switch. I was hopeful that her next session at the Aphasia Center would give similar results. Another of my hesitations about QLI was that Lauren didn't have the ability to tell me specific things about her day. If there was someone she didn't care for, or if something was bothering her, she couldn't inform me. I prayed this next session at the Aphasia Center would make things easier for her at QLI by helping her speech improve.

That summer Dave and I were celebrating twenty-five years of marriage. We wanted to do something special but were afraid to leave Lauren at home with her siblings. They already proved their incompetence. Basically, their blatant incompetence awarded them all with a once in a lifetime, seven-day cruise to the Caribbean.

A few months before our cruise, Lauren's doctor tried to transition her slowly off of her anti-seizure medications. I was nervous to make the switch, but the medication was causing increasing anger issues, especially toward her siblings. Her injury was a group effort and I had to make decisions based on all of us. Lauren's anger was not only affecting her quality of life but the well-being of our whole household.

Keeping up with schedules in our family was always complicated. We had over three times the number of children as parents. Throwing in brain injury made things extra interesting. Life didn't slow down when Lauren got hurt. Valentine's Day of 2015 landed on the same day as the Mardi Gras parade in downtown St. Louis. Maggie had high school placement testing and Shannon was meeting friends at Sam's house for *pre-gaming* before heading downtown for the parade. *Pre-game* apparently means drink for free. Since Sam's house was on the way to Maggie's school, I asked Shannon to drop Maggie off for testing and bring Lauren with her to hang out with Sam (she was past the age of pre-gaming). Dave and I had a parent meeting after Maggie's testing. Even though Maggie was our sixth daughter to attend this school (a private, all-girls Catholic high school), we felt we should both go. Maggie had been pushed aside for the last couple of years. We wanted to show her that we knew this was an exciting time for her, and both of her parents cared.

Dave and I were approaching the school when Sam called. Lauren had a five-minute seizure. This was not unexpected due to the medication change, but still scary. On the redirected way to Sam's house I called a friend and tearfully asked her to explain to Maggie why we weren't there and to drop Maggie off at our empty house after the parent meeting. I hated that she no longer had a normal childhood. Dealing with seizures was typical and her needs were always placed on the back burner. Ten minutes later, Lauren had another seizure. EMS was already there and administered medication to stop the seizure activity. I arrived as the second seizure was winding down, which marked the official end to the pregame party. As Dave and I walked in, Shannon's friends were sitting around the dining room table looking shell-shocked, a few even had tear-streaked faces. They were now officially initiated into the "I Hate Seizures" club.

After our ER visit, Lauren's doctor removed the new medication and put her back on her original seizure medication and referred us to an epilepsy specialist. This new specialist explained that breakthrough seizures were common during the transitional time. He felt we should try the new medication again and if we had break through seizures we would increase the new medication until we arrived at the correct dosage.

The medication transition is not a quick process, normally at least four to six weeks as we decrease the old and increase the new. We decided it would be best to wait until after our family cruise. That would put the end of the transition time in July. Lauren and I would then be in Florida, which wasn't ideal since I wouldn't have help. But we couldn't put it off any longer, as we would be in Omaha in August, and had no idea how long we would be at QLI. Life doesn't slow down or stop for medicine changes.

Our family cruise was scheduled for mid-June. Before the cruise, the kids kept asking me if I bought Dave an anniversary present. Each time I would laugh and tell them *I* was his anniversary present, what more could he want?

The first day of the cruise I found out why they kept encouraging me to get him a *real* gift. Dave had (with the help of the girls) bought me a gift for each day of the cruise. He has always been a hopeless romantic, while I am the practical one that preferred he didn't waste money on stupid stuff. Back when we were dating, gas stations sold single red roses. Dave brought me one of those dumb roses every single week. They had a staple through the stem attached to their plastic packaging. The staple made the rose droop and die much quicker. One day I asked him if he would mind buying me a pack of cigarettes instead of a rose? Instead, he just stopped buying roses, and thankfully years later I eventually stopped smoking.

His romantic gestures continued throughout our marriage. Sometimes I felt he only did sweet things to prove to the kids that their mother was a naggy witch. They always witnessed my eye rolls when he would walk in the house with prizes for everyone.

On the last night of our cruise, Dave handed me a ring box. I knew before I opened it what was inside. He had mentioned several times through the years that he wanted to get me a bigger diamond for my wedding ring. I had no interest in an upgrade. I loved my modest ring It was a reminder of where we had come from. My ring was a pear-shaped solitaire a little over half a carat—not a bad size for two teenage single parents.

I still remember the day we went to look at engagement rings. I had mistakenly copied the wrong address from the Yellow Pages. Here we were, two kids in love, driving aimlessly around the dangerous streets of downtown St. Louis. Soon, Fiona took over the wheel and I sat quietly in the passenger seat, wondering if I still wanted to marry the stupid ogre to my left. My eagerness to get an engagement ring outweighed my annoyance with the driver, so I sat there with my mouth shut. (First time for everything.)

As we were getting dressed for our final dinner on the cruise, I opened the ring box. Inside was a much larger, sparkly pear-shaped solitaire. I looked down at my original ring. *So long, old friend. It's been nice knowing you.*

I am thankful that after twenty-five years of marriage Dave is still a hopeless romantic, despite my protests. We laugh when we think back to our wedding day. We were two kids in love, trying our best to raise two kids. We had no clue what we were doing but tried our best. Thankfully we were too young and stupid to realize the odds were against us, and that most of our wedding guests probably thought we wouldn't make it past the first year. Somehow, we muddled through and created something pretty amazing.

In early July, Lauren and I headed back to Florida. When the anticipated breakthrough seizures began, she had been off her old seizure medication for two days and was solely taking the new drug. The first seizure came on a Friday afternoon after her first full week at the Aphasia Center. We were in the car driving home from therapy. She had another seizure after her nap. I called her epilepsy specialist after the first seizure; they increased her dosage.

The next day was rough. Lauren had two seizures by mid-morning. I called the doctor back and it took several hours for them to respond. This time they prescribed a little white pill that was designed to stop a seizure quickly by dissolving on her tongue. I was in a Walgreens pharmacy drive-thru waiting on the medication when her third seizure of the day started. By the time I got the medication, it had stopped. I called the doctor back again and let the answering service know that I needed a call back right away. This was getting scary and I had serious doubts about this new medication. I felt completely alone and helpless.

When they called back, he suggested we go to the ER. I was annoyed. Why didn't they suggest that after the *second* seizure? Lauren's body had been through so much, now I was grappling with the decision of whether I should take her to a big hospital in Tampa or the small community hospital only a few miles away? I hated being the sole person in charge of these types of decisions. When I signed up for motherhood, this was never in the contract. Technically I never actually signed up for motherhood. Does anyone voluntarily sign up at seventeen?

I was terribly afraid of a seizure happening while I was on the highway, so I opted for the closest hospital. As we pulled into its parking lot another seizure began. I drove us right up in front of the double doors and laid on my horn until nurses rushed out to help.

Lauren had six seizures in two days.

I was on the verge of a nervous breakdown.

Why were we doing this? Because she gained a little weight and yelled at her siblings? What was wrong with me? Enough was enough. We went back to a low dose of her original medication and continued on with the new one.

By Monday morning, Lauren rebounded well and was back to working hard at the Aphasia Center. I was anxious to wrap up her speech program and go home.

Lauren had been working on more complex language skills, including texting, and I was working on not having a complete nervous breakdown.

When her program was complete, we only had a couple of weeks before the two of us moved to Omaha.

Right before the cruise, I finished my first cluster of college classes, earning three As. I was pretty proud of myself. When I was young, my mother prayed for Cs. My husband, on the other hand, would have been mortified if he earned a B+. Thankfully most of our kids are more like their father…emphasis on *most* (you know who you are). Since I had no way of knowing how long Lauren's treatment in Omaha would last, I signed up for online classes.

I had been in contact with the QLI admissions director in regard to details about Lauren's new room and wall measurements. I don't think they realized the lengths I was willing to go to make Lauren's room feel homey. While Lauren spent her days working hard in Florida, I was spending hours on Pinterest and Etsy. I ordered a large monogram wall hanging to go behind Lauren's bed, a warm comforter, and several decorative items for her nightstand and dresser. Her bathroom was tougher to convert. It looked like an old nursing home bathroom, the toilet surrounded by safety bars and the sink was a plain white porcelain square with exposed pipes. There was even a metal rectangular paper towel dispenser I planned to cover up. I asked someone at QLI to measure the height and width of the sink for me. They had no way of knowing how obnoxious Colleen Murphy Interior Design could be. Once I knew the dimensions, I made a sink skirt out of fabric that hid the pipes. Porcelain isn't an easy surface to work with, but I found some extra strength adhesive Velcro strips at the fabric store. Decorative plastic containers would hold her toothpaste, hairbrush, and makeup. Instead of any institutional one-ply horror, I planned on supplying her with soft rolls of two-ply Charmin every week, one of my personal non-negotiables. I always travel with my own toilet paper. My family tells me I'm ridiculous, yet none of them use the hotel toilet paper when given a choice. If Lauren was going to live in an inpatient facility, I was determined to do whatever it took to make sure it didn't *feel* like a facility.

I chose my new apartment partly because it was near a bike trail. Dave offered to drive all of our stuff, including my bike to Omaha. He hated it when I was gone but agreed that I needed to be with Lauren. Dave was becoming accustomed to his Mr. Mom duties and the kids actually preferred his grocery shopping over mine. He and the kids went on a road trip with all our stuff as Lauren and I flew because Lauren's road trip days came to a screeching halt back in 2014 when we drove to Alabama for Erin's college graduation.

Lauren threw up seventeen times in the car on that infamous drive. I know because I counted. The gas light had come on when we were a few miles away from Erin's school. Dave didn't want to stop since we were so close. All he wanted was to get out of our car and away from the sounds and smells of someone retching. We visited with Erin for a bit before heading to our rented condo on the beach at nearby Dauphin Island. I thought it would be nice for Ryan and Maggie to play at the beach during our down time. On our way to Dauphin Island we ran out of gas while on a deserted, windy country road. We'd forgotten that we still needed gas. Dave was driving when he saw the warning on our dash: "Engine shutting down."

I decided to hold my tongue for once as I sat in our hot, vomit-smelling car, waiting for Dave and Ryan to return with gas from one of the many gas stations we had passed a few miles back.

Two days later we headed for home with our new graduate. Fifty miles outside of Mobile our car began to overheat. We were unable to use the air conditioning for most of the ride home. Somewhere between Mobile, Alabama and St. Louis, Missouri I briefly considered trading in the car along with Fiona for a few airline tickets and a bag of boiled peanuts.

That road trip marked the official end to Lauren Murphy road trips.

Unfortunately, one of us (Dave) would need to drive all of our stuff to Omaha. Lauren and I would be there for several months, so a few suitcases wouldn't cut it. Dave and the kids arrived in Omaha a few minutes before Lauren and I landed. My apartment complex was fairly new, and the furnished apartment came underwhelmingly decorated. I didn't have the energy or desire to put the same effort in decorating my new place as I did for Lauren. The ugly brown comforter on the bed was depressing and the pillows sucked. The bright white built-in shelves surrounding the TV were almost blinding and completely empty—no pictures of loved ones or cute decorations. They served as a painful reminder that in a little over twenty-four hours my apartment would be as empty as my shelves. Lauren would be moving into an obnoxiously decorated room across town and the rest of my family was headed home to continue living life without me.

Chapter Fifteen

CORNHUSKERS

L auren wasn't officially moving into QLI until Monday morning, but we moved most of her stuff in on the preceding Saturday. Decorating her room was a family affair. We all wanted Lauren to feel our love and a little piece of home in her new digs. There was a whiteboard on the wall next to her bedroom door, whereon all of her siblings wrote messages and wished her luck on her new adventure.

Sunday afternoon, all but Lauren and I went home to St. Louis. In my new Omaha apartment, the cable wasn't hooked up correctly, so Lauren and I spent the rest of our Sunday hanging out quietly, alone with our thoughts. I downloaded the movie *Crash Reel* on iTunes to watch on my laptop, hoping Lauren would be interested. *Crash Reel* was the story of Olympic hopeful Kevin Pearce and his battle back from a traumatic brain injury.

Five minutes in, Lauren fell asleep. I sat next to her and watched her sleep for hours. I wanted to soak it all in because the next day I would be dropping her off with strangers. This was harder than her first day of kindergarten. When she started kindergarten, if she felt scared or alone, she always had her big sister sitting in the next classroom. And her kindergarten class wasn't a boarding school. There would be no familiar faces for her at QLI; she had to do this all on her own. I was hopeful for her future yet terrified of the process.

Meanwhile, back at my apartment alone with nothing but my thoughts, I muddled through my online classes, struggling more than I anticipated. One thing I quickly learned was that online classes are not for old people. Another realization was that psychology was definitely not for me. I don't know what I expected but it wasn't memorizing which scientist came up with what theory and how the hippocampus works. I was way out of my league. Despite the fact that I felt I was too old and stupid for college, I *was* thankful to have my classes. They were a needed distraction. I missed the loud crazy chaos of the Murphy house but knew that if I took these classes at home surrounded by chaos, I would have zero chance to pass psychology.

Lauren's private room with its half bath was located in QLI's House 2. The house was modern with a shared kitchen, a dining room area, and two separate rooms for showers. Just off the kitchen area was a walk-in pantry. All the residents in House 2 had their own little section for grocery items. Routine grocery shopping was incorporated as part of the therapy program. Lauren would learn how to make lists, find her items at the store, and stick to a budget. One thing I knew for sure is that Murphy girls struggle with sticking to a budget, especially the matriarch. Dave would have been overjoyed if I sat in on the budget planning meetings. Unfortunately I was too busy learning the functions of the hippocampus.

After the first week, Lauren finished all of the evaluations needed to establish her baseline. I was invited to a meeting with all of her therapists and administration to discuss her needs and their plan for her rehabilitation. Dave was joining the meeting via conference call. This was eerily reminiscent of her big meeting at RIC. I anticipated this meeting to be slightly more pleasant.

The director opened the meeting with pleasantries and let us know how much they all already enjoyed getting to know Lauren as a person.

So far so good.

The next person to put in her two cents went straight for the jugular. She was one of the psychologists on staff and had given Lauren something called a neuro psych test earlier in the week. This test is primarily given to gauge intelligence, memory, attention, and planning abilities. The psychologist began her report by telling us that Lauren scored very low in cognition. She had only one score that landed in the normal category, but it was the very lowest score possible. She made sure to mention that had Lauren taken this test before her accident, the score would have been much higher. *Thanks, Captain Obvious!* She went on to give us an example of her cognitive deficits. "I showed her a triangle, a square, and a circle, and then asked her to point to the circle. She didn't even know what a circle was."

I sat there stunned. This was way worse than the time her fifth grade teacher told me at parent teacher conferences that Lauren was boy crazy and she talked too much.

I was silent. Obviously this woman didn't understand the complexity of receptive aphasia. I wanted to ask her if I were to show her those same shapes and asked the question in Mandarin, would she be able to answer correctly? Lauren knows what a circle is. Her *aphasia* is keeping her from understanding the question. When the psychologist finished with her depressing report, she left the meeting. I can't say I missed her.

The other therapists had a mix of good and bad things to say. There was nothing terrible, just examples like, when Lauren had PT scheduled first thing in the morning, she would dress herself in jeans and booties instead of workout clothes and tennis shoes. The rest of the team stayed for the whole meeting. I understood that if things were *perfect*, we wouldn't need to be there, but that psychologist really rubbed me the wrong way ("She didn't even know what a circle was.") That sentence echoed in my mind over and over again. Honestly, I barely paid attention to the rest of the meeting, I was so mad at myself for not defending Lauren to that woman. She may have known the exact functions of a hippocampus, but she knew nothing about aphasia or how to treat people with compassion.

The main thing I loved about QLI was their unique approach to therapy. They designed each program for the individual. Their goal was for the patient to return to their community in a capacity that makes the most sense for them. With the exception of the psychologist, everyone that Lauren encountered at QLI treated her as a real person, someone that mattered and was more than just an injury.

In Lauren's first week, as part of her life skills program, they took her off-campus for a manicure, and at the end of the week she had a blowout. In between the pampering, they made time for hard work at speech, OT, and PT. Her work ended every day at three in the afternoon, followed by activities such as movies, games, and arts and crafts for the residents in the evening. The first few nights I left before the activities started, hoping she might enjoy them. She preferred staying in her room. We eventually established a routine of me picking her up every day at 3:00 p.m. and taking her back to my apartment for a nap, dinner, and to just hang out. I loved that she napped in my bed. It helped me feel less alone at night because I could still smell her perfume on my pillow. We returned every night around 7:00 p.m. in time for her evening meds.

Each night at QLI, I would lay with Lauren in her bed and we would snuggle until she was ready to fall asleep. When our kids were little, they always climbed in our bed for mornings snuggles. When they got older, they plopped down at the end of our bed at night just to hang out and talk. Dave hated it because their peak time was never before 10:30 p.m. But I loved it. Our late-night talks were some of our best conversations. Fiona was always trying to kick them out so he could go to sleep, but we rarely listened to Fiona.

I hated leaving Lauren alone in her room at night. It was important to me that she never felt abandoned. Walking out the front door of House 2, along with the fifteen-minute drive back to the apartment, was the hardest part of each day. Alone in the car was where I allowed myself time to cry. I wasn't nearly as sad as when I was alone in my Chicago apartment, but I still didn't consider myself in a happy place.

Back at home, I was missing Ryan and Maggie's first day school for the third year in a row. Dave made sure he took crappy photos each year, so I didn't feel so left out. This year I would also be missing Maggie's first homecoming. Her older sisters helped her pick out a dress and took care of her hair and makeup.

I felt helpless, I was hundreds of miles away from my kids and other people were stepping in to help in my absence. For the first time, I was primarily only in charge of myself. My identity for the last twenty-five plus years was trying to be a good mom and taking care of my family. Lately I felt like I was disconnected to everyone, and as time went on, I worried Dave and the kids would become so well-adjusted they would no longer need me.

Looking back, I know how ridiculous that was. Dave is the most helpless individual on the planet. *Of course he needed me.* He can't even figure out how to order a pizza by himself.

In other news, Courtney shared with me that Lauren's old boyfriend met her for coffee to tell her that he was looking at engagement rings for his current girlfriend. I knew that he had moved on. He waited six months before he began dating again. Part of me understood while the other part of me felt that Lauren was worth the wait. *She would recover.* The fact that he had enough respect to meet with Courtney to tell her his plans made me grieve all over again for what could have been.

I decided against telling Lauren. To be honest, I wasn't sure that she would even understand. A month or so later, Erin saw on Instagram that Lauren's ex was engaged. She FaceTimed me at my apartment and blurted out the news, assuming that I had told Lauren it was coming. (I had told the rest of the family.) Lauren's mouth dropped, and she then she said, "He's engaged. He was not supportive to me with my cancer."

Erin immediately burst into tears when she saw how upset the news made Lauren. I . . . kind of giggled. Aphasia can be funny. Lauren got her point across, even if she was way off. I ended the call so I could explain things to Lauren, especially the fact that she *didn't* ever have cancer. The beauty of brain injury (is there really beauty in brain injury) is that within an hour, Lauren was over the shock and had probably already forgotten.

—

One of the things Lauren was learning at QLI was something they called errorless learning. The main concept is establishing a routine. When she wakes up, she brushes her teeth, washes her face, gets dressed, puts on her makeup etc. *always in the same order.* Her keys to her room and purse always go in the same place. This was particularly helpful for Lauren because it allowed her brain to rest. All of her things have a specific place and her day is set to a specific order. The method is designed to keep her from making mistakes. Lauren was responding really well to this way of learning and I was thrilled to see her progress in such a short amount of time.

Two of Lauren's high school friends flew in to visit her on the weekend of her birthday. The four of us went to dinner downtown. While we were gone, a bouquet of flowers were delivered to Lauren's room. We were all dying to know who they were from, but Lauren kept us all in suspense. She refused to look at the card until she put her keys and her purse in the correct spot, washed her face, brushed her teeth, and put on her pajamas. Nothing would make her deter from her routine. Once she was ready for bed, she read the card. The flowers were from Courtney. Errorless learning is serious stuff.

Lauren was also learning to rely heavily on her iPhone calendar. She enjoyed knowing what was next in her day and felt more in control of her own life. She had spent over two and a half years relying on other people to direct her day. This was putting more control back in Lauren's hands.

QLI had the look and feel of a small college campus. Many even refer to the program as brain injury college. It didn't take long before Lauren was independently moving around campus. She checked her schedule at the end of therapy to find out where to go next, just like a regular college student.

Lauren and I flew home to St. Louis in October so she could attend a Taylor Swift concert with all of her sisters. After the concert, the girls were invited backstage to meet Taylor. Last time Lauren and Taylor were together, Lauren was in a coma. When the girls arrived backstage along with all the other meet and greet fans, Taylor's staff let them know that photos were only done in groups, and then Taylor would sign a quick autograph.

Taylor called my girls over first and specifically requested a picture with just her and Lauren. She seemed genuinely pleased and shocked to see how well Lauren was doing and how good she looked. Lauren had her iPad with her in her purse. One of the girls suggested Lauren ask Taylor to autograph the back of her case. Instead of a standard autograph, Taylor wrote:

> *Lauren,*
> *I can't begin to tell you how proud I am of you. I hope you always remember how brave you've been. You're a miracle.*
> *Taylor*

Before the concert, I wasn't sure if Lauren would have the stamina to make it through the whole show. The girls knew there was a high possibility they would be leaving before the concert was over; they were well versed in Lauren's Irish goodbyes. Thankfully, Lauren pushed through, and the girls created a memory together that will last a lifetime.

Lauren and I flew back to Omaha the very next day. The weather in Omaha was starting to get colder. The changing seasons somehow made being away from home sting a little bit more. I turned on the apartment's heat and could smell the burnt dust from the furnace. This familiar smell previously reminded me of home. Feeling the warm air coming from the vents always made me feel safe and warm. Now it was just an ugly reminder of all the time I was missing away from home.

There's a floor heat vent in our kitchen that the kids would fight over when they were little. They liked to sit on it while eating their cereal in the morning. Ryan called it the "heat bench." To this day, on chilly mornings, he occasionally sits there with a bowl of cereal.

While I was living in Omaha, Maggie earned the nickname "Little Deb" from her friends at school. Now that Dave was in charge of grocery shopping, Ryan and Maggie survived solely on Little Debbie baked goods. Dave stopped at the grocery store every night for his nightly ritual of a rotisserie chicken and a salad from the salad bar for himself, while Ryan and Maggie alternated between honey buns, Swiss Rolls, and Cosmic Brownies for dinner. The dinner ritual was the same every night. It seemed as if Dave was catching on to errorless learning too.

———

Lauren and I flew home for a few days in November to celebrate Thanksgiving. Our flight was delayed, and Lauren was struggling with sitting still. The Omaha airport is really small and once you pass security your options in the terminal are very limited. I was going to need to get creative in order to keep Lauren sitting. I opened my computer and pulled up all the pictures I had from Lauren's accident and recovery. We went through hundreds of photos while we sat there killing time. She seemed genuinely interested in each image and after several minutes she looked at me with a very serious look on her face and asked, "Where were you?"

I wasn't in any of the photos, so she assumed I wasn't there.

I wanted to tell her, "I was busy painfully balancing on a metal side rail, holding your head up to keep you from choking on your own vomit."

Instead I laughed and told her I took all of the pictures.

Once we finally made it back to St. Louis, my first order of business was finding out what was needed at the grocery store. To begin, I opened the door to the pantry, where it was safe to say we had plenty of chips and snack cakes but little else. It felt like I was starting from scratch. My kitchen was no longer my kitchen. I felt more like a guest—a guest who didn't get access to the best towels or linens, but a guest whose bathroom had been stripped of every last bottle of body wash, shampoo, conditioner, and razor by the vermin that lived down the hall.

At Thanksgiving dinner, we all went around the table saying what we were thankful for. When it was Dave's turn, he made a joke about how he was thankful his wife refers to her apartment in Omaha as her "home." We all laughed. It drove Dave crazy whenever I would say something like, "I left my favorite sweatshirt at home" or "I need to remember to bring that home with me when I leave."

He would correct me every time by saying, "*This* is your home."

In my defense, it was much easier than saying, "I left my favorite sweatshirt at *my temporary housing in Omaha.*"

Now that I knew it bothered him, I made sure to refer to it as my home every chance I got. I had to keep him on his toes!

———

Dave and the kids visited us several times during our time in Omaha. It made my time there much more bearable. On the weekends that we didn't have visitors, we were running out of things to explore. Lauren was having Nordstrom withdrawal. Every Saturday morning, I would pick her up and she would type "Nordstrom" into her phone. She was convinced Omaha had a Nordstrom department store. (It doesn't.) What she found was a dentist in Omaha named Dr. Nordstrom. Every single weekend she pulled up his name. If he would have had Saturday hours, I might have dropped her off on his doorstep and let him try to explain it to her.

QLI was working on correcting some of Lauren's behavior issues. If she wanted to talk to someone, she would walk up (even if they were talking with someone else) and interrupt, or she would walk into an office with a closed door without knocking. She acted as if rules didn't apply to her. She was still highly social but was also highly socially inappropriate. It was common for her to reach for someone's hand while they were talking or for her to place her hand on someone's arm if she was talking to them. She was starving for an emotional attachment that she could no longer receive verbally; touch was a way for her to feel connected to people. Although I understood why she did it, it was important for her to know that it was not appropriate for her to rest her hand on the upper arm of the lady seated next to her on an airplane.

When Lauren first began finding her words and speaking, she would tell everyone she encountered that she loved them. It was really sweet in the beginning. Friends and family were thrilled to hear those three little words. It began to get out of hand when she was professing her love at the same time she was writing those three thousand dollar checks. She loved *everyone*: waiters, doctors, therapists, and my personal favorite, telemarketers. I knew I had to find a way to get through to her that she couldn't possibly love *all* of these people.

It was hard to watch when I would see Lauren reach for one of her therapists' hands while she was interacting with them. They would tuck their hands in their pockets and ignore her outstretched hand to keep her from making contact. Part of me wanted to tell them to stop being so mean, but I knew she needed to relearn social appropriateness and they were helping her. Lauren had to learn how to navigate her way through life. Her lack of filter and body language often put us in awkward situations. This was why we were in Omaha. I needed to let go and let the experts show me how to help her. Hurt feelings had no place in her rehabilitation.

Chapter Sixteen

MORE INDEPENDENCE

By the end of December, QLI was talking about moving Lauren from House 2 to an apartment across campus. It had its own private entrance, kitchen area, living area, and full bath. They wanted to see how Lauren would do with more independence. The plan was to move all of her stuff to the new apartment while we were home over the Christmas break. She would start fresh in a new space after the first of the year.

Another change would be me stepping back a bit and only coming to visit Lauren on the weekends. I knew my being there made her feel secure and loved but it wasn't doing much for her independence. I needed to back away but wasn't willing to leave town without being absolutely sure she would be okay on her own.

I decided I would remain in Omaha on *standby* all of January. I only visited Lauren Fridays night through Sunday. This wasn't easy and required me to take many retail therapy trips to Marshalls or TJ Maxx. (Sorry Dave—just be grateful Omaha didn't have a Nordstrom.) Beginning in February, I would be flying home every Monday morning and return to Omaha on Friday night.

There are only two things in this world that I cannot tolerate: onions and being cold. Okay, maybe *three* things. I also don't like it when Dave says mean things about Rick Springfield.

When Lauren and I returned to Omaha after Christmas, the temperature hovered around negative three degrees. I wasn't prepared for my face to freeze off every time I got out of the car.

Lauren's new apartment had an electronic keypad. Part of her therapy was remembering the PIN to enter her apartment. I am all in for progress but was it really that great of an idea to teach a person with memory issues a four-digit PIN in the dead of winter. We would stand there next to her keypad as Lauren tried to remember the code. She had it written in her phone in case she forgot. If only she could remember *where* it was located in her phone, that might have been a little more helpful. I knew that I shouldn't step in to help, but my God, couldn't they have tried this in September? Many times, we would have to walk around the building, through a foot of snow, to get indoors through a different entrance.

At home in St. Louis, I would love watching the snow fall. I would sit in my favorite spot on the couch, wrapped in a warm, fuzzy blanket, drinking my morning coffee watching Dave through the front window shovel the driveway and walkways. In Omaha, I would also sit in my apartment watching the snow fall out the front window . . . as I sat on my ugly beige, scratchy couch, knowing I would have to clean off my car and drive in the mess if I wanted to visit Lauren. I didn't even own a broom. Isn't it an unwritten rule that men clean snow off of cars, cut the grass, and take the kids trick or treating? I knew that I needed to stop acting like such a baby. I was on my own and it was time for me to put on my big girl pants.

I loved my daughter more than I hated the cold.

I could do this.

———

Lauren adjusted well to her new apartment. She kept it neat and even did a little cooking during therapy. One area of concern was her inability to independently find things to do to fill her downtime. If she was bored, she would walk around campus trying to find someone who would take her somewhere. Entertaining herself was problematic. Aphasia made watching TV pointless because she couldn't understand the dialogue and she couldn't read. Listening to music seemed to be the only outlet for her. Aphasia was the sucker punch that made everything immensely more challenging.

Thankfully, I was no longer referred to as Jason, but I dreamt of a day that I could have a real conversation with my daughter where she could share with me her thoughts and feelings. I wondered if that would ever be possible and if maybe I was setting our goals too high.

QLI tried to cover everything in regard to independence. Safety issues would need to be re-taught. Looking both ways when she crossed a street was high on the list, but also things like knowing not to open the door to a stranger and knowing what to do in the case of a fire. Her therapist scheduled a surprise fire drill one afternoon after she finished therapy. The fire alarm went off during Lauren's naptime. Her therapist stood outside the door for several minutes waiting for Lauren to react. After five or six minutes passed, she used her key and went inside. Lauren was sitting on the edge of her bed putting on high-heeled boots. Clearly, she failed her fire safety test, but it should be noted that she picked out fabulous shoes.

Despite the failed fire safety test, Lauren was doing well in her apartment. We were coming to the end of her independent living program. Her discharge was scheduled for early March. Her therapists helped us come up with a plan that would benefit Lauren while transitioning back to life at home. Lauren would participate in speech therapy through Skype with the Aphasia Center four days a week. Routine and consistency at home was important for Lauren to remain successful. In theory that sounded great, but in reality it proved to be a bit challenging. While she was at QLI, a therapist could call in sick or cancel and someone else would take their spot. Regardless, her schedule remained the same. We didn't have that luxury. Our family was too big and too active to not have hiccups in our daily schedule.

One of the best things we have done to help Lauren took place back in December of 2014. I had been taking Lauren to the gym with very little success. Lauren would head for the door after spending five minutes on the elliptical machine. Truth be told, I was fine with leaving (I hate to exercise), but I knew Lauren would benefit from the many benefits of exercise. I also knew that I was in over my head. Per Erin's suggestion, Sam put a message out on Lauren's CaringBridge site, asking if anyone was interested in becoming Lauren's trainer. Jaime responded, and the rest was history.

We did not know Jaime prior to Lauren's accident. She was married with three little boys. After her third baby was born, she left her job as a speech therapist to stay home with her kids. She also teaches fitness classes. Once we met, I knew she would be perfect. She understood aphasia and with three little boys at home, she obviously knew how to think on her feet.

Jaime had a strong personality and knew how to handle Lauren. She pushed her physically as well as verbally. For instance, while they ran at local parks, Lauren was expected to verbally greet each runner or walker they passed. And Lauren wasn't allowed to repeat the same greeting twice. Lauren's go-to was always "Good morning." Jaime was tough. She pushed Lauren to be better and we loved her for that. I still remember the day Jaime texted me and said, "We just had our first fight."

I laughed and told her, "Welcome to the club."

———

Now that we were back home, Lauren and Jaime resumed their workouts, which was a good thing.

A week after Lauren's discharge from QLI, Lauren and I flew to Orange County, California to meet Courtney for a wedding of a college friend of theirs. Courtney was staying in the hotel with us. Dave flew in a day or two later. Courtney was flying back home to New York on Sunday, but we planned to stay through Monday so we could visit Cedars-Sinai and Dr. Chen.

Once I knew we were coming to LA, I wanted to buy Dr. Chen a gift for Lauren to give him. What do you buy the man who was responsible for saving your daughter's life? There wasn't enough money in the world for me to buy him a gift worthy of how much love and admiration I felt for him. I found a company online that etches photos into glass paperweights. I used the photo of Dr. Chen's hands holding Lauren's prosthetic skull. Under the etching of the photo was an inscription that read "Thanks for bringing your *A* game."

On Saturday we did a little sightseeing. Even though I spent months living smack dab in the middle of Beverly Hills, the only thing I ever saw was the hospital and McDonald's. Our first order of business was to drive out to Malibu, home of Rick Springfield. He wasn't home. I know, because I checked. Just kidding. I didn't *really* go to his house (mainly because I didn't know how to find it), but we did walk along the Malibu Pier and down on the beach.

Next, we headed toward LA. We drove past my old apartment. Lauren and I jumped out and had Dave take a picture of us in the driveway. A few miles away was the infamous intersection where Lauren was hit, Hollywood Boulevard and Fuller. I wasn't sure how I felt revisiting the scene of the accident, but I felt it was important for Lauren to see it for herself.

Lauren was hit by a Mercedes on Hollywood Boulevard. Somehow the circumstances didn't shock me. If anyone could find a way to turn a critical injury into something reminiscent of a movie scene, it was her. Watching her stand at that street corner flexing her muscles was a powerful moment for me. It was as if she was standing tall and showing the world her superhuman strength. I stood next to her on that sidewalk and said a quick prayer of thanks—a prayer for Lauren, a prayer for the driver, the witnesses, the first responders, and for all who have helped Lauren on her road to recovery. I looked at a specific section of the pavement. I have a photo of that exact spot at home from the police report. There is an X marking the spot where my baby girl landed. Three years ago, she was in that spot, a broken, bloody mess. Today she was standing tall, full of hope and promise.

Our next stop was just down the road to the Hollywood Walk of Fame. Rick Springfield received his long overdue Hollywood Star the exact same weekend I was driving to Alabama holding Lauren's puke bucket on the way to Erin's graduation. Since we were right down the street, I had to take a peek. I brought Windex and paper towels with me to polish his star. Just kidding, I'm not *that* crazy, although I did sit on the filthy sidewalk and pose for a photo.

Our LA hotel was fifteen miles from the hospital. With traffic it took us over two hours to arrive. I had always heard that LA traffic was terrible, but never experienced it firsthand. When I lived there, I only drove back and forth from the hospital to my nearby apartment. About thirty minutes into our drive, Fiona arrived. Apparently Fiona didn't like my choice in hotels. Luckily there was an outlet mall next to our hotel. There was no way I would be getting back in the car with Fiona. We finished the rest of our day with a little shopping. After our adventurous two-hour traffic jam, Dave said to me, "I don't care what it costs, cancel our room for Sunday night and find us something closer to the hospital."

Sunday afternoon we checked into The Beverly Hilton on Wilshire Boulevard. When will that man ever learn? "I don't care what it costs" is probably not the smartest thing he has ever said to me.

Monday morning, Lauren had her hair blown out at the Beverly (thankfully Dave was in an *I don't care what it costs* kind of mood) while Dave ran out to pick up breakfast, Lauren was getting all glammed up. We were meeting at Dr. Chen's office before heading to the ICU.

When Dr. Chen walked in to greet us, I immediately got teary-eyed. Lauren handed him her gift, gave him a hug, and told him thank you. We took a few pictures before we headed toward Saperstein Critical Care Tower. We went the back way, the way the doctors come in. Nothing looked familiar. When we walked through the double doors leading to the ICU, I wanted to start skipping. The last time I was there I was always scared and sad. This day I was joyful.

Remembering Lauren in bed with a huge part of her skull missing and her head shaved was a stark contrast to present day. We were walking into the ICU (some of us skipping) and Lauren looked like she had just stepped out of the salon (she had) and was ready to walk the red carpet. Many of the people who cared for Lauren were there that morning. Once word got around that Lauren was on the unit, a small gleeful crowd gathered around her. Several of the staff members had watery eyes upon seeing Lauren standing in the doorway just like Dave and I. Becky, the nurse who took care of Lauren on her first night in the ICU, was there. Theresa, the nurse who would shave Lauren's head every other day (to keep her bandage from coming up), was there too. Now Theresa could see Lauren's beautiful head of thick, healthy, shiny hair. Dr. Yen was no longer at Cedars but many of the people that were in that first meeting led by Dr. Yen were present. It was hard to believe that many of them were the same people in the meeting where I asked if I needed to fly my kids to California to say goodbye to Lauren.

Lauren seemed slightly overwhelmed. She had no memory of any of these people and they were all absolutely ecstatic to see her. We only stayed about ten minutes; the neuro ICU is a serious place and they all had patients to care for. We posed for a group photo and headed toward the ICU waiting room. This was the room I would sit in when I felt overwhelmed in Lauren's room. It was where I was when I met the driver that hit Lauren and where Dave spent most of his time because seeing his daughter so broken wasn't easy. The back wall of the waiting room was all windows. Feeling the warm sun reflecting off those windows reminded me of how the sun would warm my tear-streaked face as I would sit motionless in the hard-plastic chairs placed in front of the window. Many times, I would stand facing the window so others wouldn't see my flood of tears. I remembered there was a painted mural on a building right outside the window and under the mural was written "It's a cruel world."

I would look at the sign every day and be in total agreement. Today the side of the building was painted with something different—an ad for an expensive watch. I looked out that window and thought, *I was wrong. The world isn't cruel. The world is beautiful.* Then I wondered, *Maybe Dave should buy me a new watch.*

After a brief moment or two soaking up the atmosphere of the waiting room, Dr. Chen walked us downstairs and outside. It was bittersweet as we left the Saperstein Critical Care Tower for the very last time.

For old times' sake, we ate lunch in the hospital cafeteria. After lunch, I stopped at Starbucks to see if they would get my name right (they didn't). Dave and Lauren went to walk around campus while I found my favorite bench to sit and enjoy my tea. This time, I didn't cry. I was feeling proud. I wanted to tell everyone that walked past how incredible my daughter was. On paper, she should not have survived her accident, let alone walked back through those doors three years later wearing high heels. I was so grateful for Cedars-Sinai. Had this accident happened anywhere else, she may not have survived.

For Dave and me, the visit to Cedars was overwhelming. For Lauren, it was unfamiliar. She had seen pictures and she understood how serious things had been, but for her, Cedars was unceremonious. She was probably wondering why her parents made her eat crappy hospital food for lunch.

Lauren has no memory of her time at Cedars, or RIC, or her many months of outpatient therapy. She lost a full two years of memories. Had I known she wouldn't remember, I wouldn't have spent that first year shaving her legs and doing her hair and makeup every day. As we drove away from Cedars, I quietly reflected on the events of the day and how far Lauren had come. Many times throughout her recovery I felt as if things were never going to get better. I needed this day to remind me of how great things already were and that the best was yet to come.

Later, we drove to the airport. This time we would not be leaving California in a private air ambulance. My girl would be walking down the jetway just like everyone else. Today, life was the complete opposite of cruel.

Key 4: Work Hard

Every single day, Lauren works hard on her recovery. Running is something that makes Lauren feel like her old self. She has worked really hard to build her endurance. Lauren runs with her trainer Jaime, as well as her dad. Together, they have completed thirty-five 5Ks.

Once, a seizure happened three-tenths of a mile from the finish. Lauren ended up in the back of an ambulance with back-to-back seizures; eventually needing so much medication, she was knocked out for several hours.

It often takes Lauren a few days to feel well again. Three days later, she insisted I take her back to the running course so she could complete the last few minutes of the race. Her work ethic never ceases to amaze me.

Reading is still one of Lauren's biggest hurdles. Imagine having a master's degree and losing the ability to read or write. For Lauren, speech therapy is exhausting. Despite how impossible it feels, she spends hours each week trying. The progress has been painfully slow, but Lauren remains focused and determined. She has signs all over her bathroom mirror that say, "I will get my words back." Regaining her full ability to speak is a lofty goal, but as her head cheerleader, it is my job to tell her that she can definitely do it, and more importantly, I too need to believe it can and will happen.

We all know hard work pays off. Still, many of us (myself included) get frustrated and quit when we don't see fast results. Losing weight, getting a job promotion, studying for a test . . . none of us like doing things that don't come easy. If only brain injury recovery—or any other obstacle standing in our way—had a fast track. There is no quick fix; hard work takes time and can be painstakingly slow. Stay the course!

Chapter Seventeen

HALL OF FAME

I am the queen of flying by the seat of her pants, so establishing a consistent routine was a bit of a challenge for me. But I was willing to do whatever was necessary to help Lauren recover.

Too often my kids missed out on activities because I was a disorganized hot mess. Years ago, I sent my youngest daughter, Maggie, to school on the wrong day in a full nun habit costume. Her second-grade class was learning about saints. During one of their prayer services the kids were all to dress like their favorite saint. Now that I was a full-time working mom, I had a ton of guilt. I was determined to make sure Maggie had a fierce costume. (Can you have a fierce nun costume?) Anyway, I went to the fabric store and got to work. Mary Margaret Murphy would have the best Saint Margaret Mary Alacoque costume in all the land.

I worked day and night trying to make that costume. Honestly, I had no clue what I was doing. The first version I made was my size. I have no idea how that happened. I pretty much cut it in in half and started over. Somehow, I managed to make it look *somewhat* like a black and white nun's habit.

The morning of the prayer service I proudly helped her get dressed. Her hot pink Crocs were the perfect touch. Her school uniform and shoes were folded neatly in her backpack so she could change after the prayer service.

Maggie got out of the car in the carpool lane and I recognized a problem right away. One of the teachers shot us a confused look. We are the type of family

183

that pulls up at the sound of the morning bell. By now dozens of miniature saints should have already arrived. As I pulled away, I knew I had completely messed up second grade saint day. We had the wrong week; the prayer service was the following week. Holy heck our 401(k) wasn't even close to being big enough to cover all the therapy my children would need due to their incompetent parents. (Okay, their incompetent mother.)

If only Maggie could have been fortunate enough to have had the new and improved, plan ahead, write-it-down-in-a-calendar kind of mom. *That* version of me would have showed up on the correct day.

Even while on vacation in California for the wedding, I added things to Lauren's calendar throughout the day to make it easier for her. For instance, one afternoon she was shopping with Courtney and she had a lot of anxiety wondering when she would be able to meet back up with her father and me. Lauren called me to see what time I was meeting them. I told her we were having lunch and would meet her at 3:00 p.m. but also added, *meet mom at 3:00 p.m.* on her calendar (we have joint access). The more specifics she had, the more control she felt over her day. I never took the time to stop and think how hard that must have been for her. She had no control over anything and even if I told her our plans earlier in the day, there was a pretty good chance that she already forgot.

———

Dave and I were excitedly going to be grandparents for the first time. My oldest daughter, Sam, and her husband, John, were expecting their first baby in November. Thankfully, Lauren no longer called me Grandma, just in time for me to become an actual grandma. Sam found out she was having a boy. We couldn't have been happier—especially future Uncle Ryan, who was tired of dealing with all the crazy Murphy girls. It was time for another male in the family.

Danny was born a few days before Halloween. Life was good.

It was better than good; it was fantastic.

On Thanksgiving we had so much to be thankful for. Having a new baby around helped take the focus off of just Lauren, which was a good thing. She did not need to be babied. It was time for her to take charge of her own recovery.

The last time we saw Lauren's neurologist, he lowered her dose of Prozac. Now that we had made it past the Thanksgiving break with all the kids home from college, I realized she needed to go back to her original dosage. There wasn't enough Prozac in the world for Lauren to live comfortably with a full house of Murphys. Lauren's brain couldn't handle noise or clutter. If someone left their shoes in the living room she acted as if they stomped on a puppy. I was constantly telling her to take it easy and reminding everyone else to pick up their stuff.

This was when I decided that our house would never be peaceful and maybe I should become a raging alcoholic. When I was young, I always had a baby to take care of—waking up early on a Saturday or Sunday morning with a hangover wasn't worth the effort. I now rarely drank. On a whim while grocery shopping, I picked up the holiday edition of Baileys Irish Cream. The bottle came in a fancy box with four glass tumblers. Every night I would pour a little Baileys on ice while I was cooking dinner. I quickly realized that I liked my family so much more when I was a little drunk. Why didn't anyone ever tell me this? By the first of the year, my cabinets were full of holiday tumblers.

Once the kids were all back in school, I resumed my boring sober life. Lauren continued to train with Jaime, and we added an additional two days of exercise with DASA (Disabled Athletes Sports Association). This helped Lauren by keeping her busy and interacting with other people every day. Lauren's speech was becoming almost conversational. She could ask and answer questions. When she wasn't angry about shoes being left in the wrong spot, she would tell jokes and interact more during family events.

One of the things we like to do at dinner is go around the table and share our high and low of the day. The Murphy kids are ferociously competitive and daily highs and lows are no exception. In the past, Lauren would just sit at the table and listen; the concept was too hard for her to understand. During a family barbecue, we went around the table as usual. When we got to Lauren, we asked her if she could tell us her high and low. She looked around at everyone and started to speak. I wasn't sure what she would say or if she understood. We always ask but normally she says nothing. This time she started circling her hand around her head and said, "All this brain damage."

Okay Lauren, your low is definitely the winner. We all laughed so hard, we cried.

Times like these were precious. Lauren never tried to participate and then, all of a sudden, she was engaged and making us all laugh.

Our kitchen table was the setting for many funny moments. The first time my son-in-law John came over for brunch, he and Sam had just started dating. All of the kids were warned to be on their best behavior. Sam actually liked this guy and he seemed normal. We knew this because we had spent one evening huddled around the computer stalking him online. With all of the girls' boyfriends, I did my research. All I needed was a name and I could find out anything. Because John played professional soccer, he had his own Wikipedia page, which made things easier. And it was impressive. We found some of his old interviews and video highlights. We stopped short of a credit and criminal background check.

The morning of the brunch, Lauren walked in our front door and headed straight to the powder room to throw up. Apparently, she had a fun night. I rolled my eyes and thought,

At least she was on time.

I was standing at my griddle working on a third batch of pancakes when I heard one of the kids say from across the table, "OMG Lauren, you have puke in your hair."

Seriously, can't we ever be normal? To this day I am not sure why John didn't head for the door and never look back. There isn't a sane Murphy in the bunch. On a side note, I just looked at his Wikipedia page again. It has him listed as 5'8". John has many gifts, but being tall isn't one of them. All I'm saying is that if he's 5'8", I weigh what my driver's license says I weigh (ninety-five pounds.).

The old Lauren wasn't the type to clean up after herself or anyone else. The new and improved Lauren was the complete opposite. She had a hard time relaxing; Lauren would do household chores like she was Cinderella. My dishwasher was unloaded every morning before I woke up, and she loved doing the laundry. In the beginning I thought it was great, but her behavior became more and more obsessive. Lauren couldn't stand for any clothes to be left behind on the laundry room floor. Every load she did was overstuffed. I would try to gently explain why it wasn't a good idea to put so many items in one load, but I might have done better talking to the wall. She also took on a new obsession with Kleenexes. Her purse held at least fifty. She kept a box next to her bed, in her bathroom, and in the kitchen. These things seemed minor compared to where she had been, but they were beginning to consume her. If it was raining, she had to have her head completely covered either by a hood on her jacket or an umbrella. She would walk across a parking lot oblivious to cars because the raindrops hitting her head made her insane. She began checking her weather app several times each day.

Lauren also developed a fascination with the mail service. Whenever the mail truck arrived, even if she was in a deep sleep, she would somehow hear the truck and bolt out of bed in time to greet the mailman. Our driveway could be covered with a sheet of ice and it wouldn't have mattered, nothing kept her from reaching the mailbox. I felt like I was constantly trying to hold back a caged lion. These impulses were so strong, she could focus on little else.

Messy tables were something that really set her off. When she was finished eating, she expected the waitress to stop what she was doing and take her plate the minute Lauren set her fork down. I was constantly trying to explain to her that she came off as rude, and that we needed to come up with a strategy to help her relax while waiting for the waitress to clear the table. Any type of party we went to, Lauren was picking up plates and cups to throw in the trash. The problem was that she didn't care if the people were finished eating. If the cup or the plate was making her crazy, it went to the trash.

As Lauren's primary caregiver, I felt like I spent most of my day telling her everything that she did wrong. I tried to find a balance and compliment her on things that she was doing well. One thing that she was doing very well was running. We had worked hard building up her stamina and endurance. In just over three years, she went from a twenty-two-minute mile to a consistent ten-minute mile. Running did not come easy for Lauren. Her brain processes things at a much slower pace, so uneven sidewalks have caused her to trip and fall many times. She had a pretty bad fall once while running with Jaime, hitting her head on the sidewalk. Jaime felt terrible and was really upset. Lauren was more upset that her Coach sunglasses got scratched. She was perfectly fine with the huge black eye that showed up on her face the next day.

Another issue of Lauren's running was overheating and dehydration. The first time it happened we were on a family vacation in Florida. Lauren got so dehydrated while running it triggered a seizure. This was the first time a seizure affected her speech. She was unable to speak clearly for several weeks. Her understanding of words was also affected. We worked so hard to help Lauren get to where she was, and now we were afraid her speech wouldn't return to baseline. Luckily after a few weeks things were much better. She would ultimately have several more seizures over the next year while running. I spoke with her epilepsy specialist at length about discontinuing running but he felt the benefits still outweighed the risks. Lauren agreed. I had my reservations.

Jaime became quite the expert in recognizing Lauren's symptoms. We have medication we can give Lauren that often prevent her seizure activity from progressing to a convulsive type of seizure. Nothing comes easy for Lauren. Sometimes it's hard for me to sit back and watch. It feels as if she can never catch a break.

In 2017, Lauren was inducted into her high school's Hall of Fame. All of the inductees give a speech after receiving their award. I wasn't sure how Lauren would feel about speaking in front of a large audience. I knew the school would be fine if a family member spoke on her behalf. I asked Lauren how she wanted to handle the evening. She had no hesitation; she would be delivering the speech herself. I figured her willingness to speak was half the battle, but it was the other half that worried me. Dave was strongly against letting her speak.

To help her write the speech, I gave her several suggestions and she would tell me whether she liked it or not. Lauren wasn't shy on opinions. The key to her speech was to keep it simple, short, and sweet. Once we came up with a solid speech, we began practicing several times a day. Reading was still very difficult for Lauren. I was hoping by repeating the speech over and over again something would stick. The odds were against us. She couldn't read and she couldn't remember most things. I thought, *How in the world is she going to pull this off?*

I knew that especially with Lauren, where there was a will, there was a way. We rolled up our sleeves and got to work. We continued to practice that speech several times every single day for months. When she rode in the car, we would turn off the radio and recite the speech over and over again. Sometimes it felt like the movie *Fifty First Dates*, each day was brand new. I would ask, "Does this sound remotely familiar?"

We would laugh and push forward. One thing I learned was that it was very helpful for Lauren to write out the speech herself. Writing the words down helped her brain remember. I typed her speech with big font and emphasized some of the harder words in bold, thinking that might be helpful, but instead we found that she did much better reading when it was her own handwriting. The week before the induction, things were finally coming together. I began to think she might actually pull this off. The plan was for Erin to go up to the podium with Lauren, to help prompt her if she got stuck.

Four days before the ceremony Lauren had a seizure while working out. She could barely say her own name. I was heartbroken for her. How was she going to deliver a three-minute speech when she couldn't even say her own name? I had a video of one of our last practice runs where she did really well. I contacted the school to see if we could play a video of her speech if things didn't improve. The problem with the video was that Lauren was wearing a t-shirt and shorts in her recorded speech and this was a formal event. Plan B was not the best solution, but it was at least a solution.

By the day of the induction her talking was a little better, but she was nowhere near her normal baseline. One of the first lines of her speech was "I graduated from Incarnate Word Academy in 2006." An hour before the ceremony, every time we practiced, she would say, "I graduated from Fontbonne University in 2006."

It was like she was stuck. She *did* go to Fontbonne for college, but this was her high school Hall of Fame induction.

Erin drove her to the ceremony in a separate car. Once they arrived Lauren had to remain with the rest of the inductees until they all processed into the theater. When Erin sat down in our section of seats, she told me Lauren practiced in the car and it was dreadful. Dave felt, even before the seizure, that it was too much for her and she shouldn't do it. Obviously, I seldom listen to Dave. I was hoping this wouldn't be one of the few times I had to admit that he was right.

Lauren processed in with the group and after they stood on stage for a few seconds she found her aisle seat next to Dave and me. She was scheduled to receive her award midway through the program. Lauren was normally in bed by 8:00 p.m. sharp; the ceremony didn't begin until 7:00 p.m. That combined with the recent seizure was a recipe for disaster. Somehow, I knew that despite the odds being against her, she would find a way to pull this off.

When the dean of students began reading her bio, my lip trembled. He knew our family well; we have sent six daughters through that school. Incarnate Word was more like a family than a school. Erin was now standing backstage waiting for Lauren to be called up before she met her at the podium. When the dean finished the bio, he went off script and got choked up as he talked about how great it was to have a front row seat to Lauren's recovery. When Lauren's name was called the auditorium erupted in applause and she received a standing ovation. As she walked proudly up to the stage in her four-inch heels, I thought, *Oh no, we didn't practice a standing ovation. I hope this doesn't throw her off.*

She eventually made her way to the podium and began to speak. We found out later that Erin's face was full of tears; the intro combined with the standing ovation triggered the waterworks. She was standing there without a Kleenex (Lauren had fifty in her purse).

Lauren took several deep breaths before she began. Once she found her groove, there was no stopping her. Erin stood to her right and would give her the first word of the sentence when she got stuck. I looked over at Dave and saw that he had tears in his eyes. Part of me wanted to say, "See, I told you so."

But instead I thought I would be a good wife and rub the back of his hair as a sign of affection (sometimes I'm nice like that). Lauren made it back to her chair after her speech and fought to stay awake for the rest of the program.

The following weeks Lauren walked with an extra skip in her step. She was proud of herself for the first time in a very long time. Even with her many deficits, she has an uncanny ability to win people over with her magnetic personality. Her story was inspiring to all those who heard it. This night was special. *Lauren* was special. She thrived in the spotlight. I knew that, eventually, she would be ready to share her story with others.

Chapter Eighteen

GRADUATING, FINALLY

By December of 2017, there was a light at the end of the tunnel. I was finally nearing the end of my college classes. I was proud to be righting a wrong and showing my kids that it's never too late to go back and fix past mistakes. My capstone course was the last requirement before graduation. The course was designed to be a culmination of everything I had learned while seeking my Communications degree.

For my final project I had several options: design a website, do a podcast, write a gazillion-page research paper, create a film, or write a business proposal. I decided to create a film about Lauren's accident and recovery. It felt only fitting since she was the main reason I started college. Immediately, I started brainstorming. I wanted to do Lauren's story justice. While putting together my outline for the movie, I thought it might be more interesting to tell *two* stories—Lauren's story and a girl named Lindsey's, who suffered a TBI in Spain a month before Lauren. I wanted to create something that would make both families proud. An honest account of brain injury, the good the bad and the ugly.

I scheduled several interviews and borrowed camera equipment from school. Although in way over my head, I was excited about the project. For the interviews, I included the girls, both sets of parents, and some of their therapists. I used several photos and videos of each girl throughout their recoveries that made great B-roll.

Days after Lauren's accident, back at Cedars-Sinai, Courtney asked if it would be okay if she took a picture of Lauren. I hesitated before telling her yes. But I told her if things didn't end well, she would need to delete the photo. I couldn't even bring myself to say *if Lauren would die.*

That awful photo is the first of many painful photos and videos that I saved on my computer. Despite how hard it is to look at, I'm thankful I have it. I deleted several photos because they were so terrible. I had no way of knowing what the future held for Lauren. I thought I was protecting her by deleting some of the hard stuff.

Thankfully, I still have a vast array of recovery videos—so much so that I had hours of footage to sift through. After many sleepless nights of editing, I was finally finished. My documentary was a little over an hour long.

———

Kelsey and I were both communication majors finishing up our last semester of school. As luck would have it, my December graduation fell on the exact same day and time as Kelsey's. Kelsey was graduating a semester early and I was graduating twenty-seven years late. Kelsey's school was three hours away, but I wasn't going to miss my daughter's graduation. I had already missed too much by taking care of Lauren, including most of her collegiate soccer games. Missing her graduation would not be an option.

One of the few games I was able to attend came close to ending the Murphy marriage. The game was in late September and it was unseasonably hot. As we left that morning, I tried to convince Lauren to wear shorts, but she insisted on wearing her black Lululemon leggings. Lauren rarely made it through any of her siblings sporting events. The excessive heat wasn't helping. Per usual, she decided to leave a few minutes after the game started. I went with her to go sit in the car while Dave stayed to watch the game. After the game, they were having a team potluck for the players and their families. The temperature was only going to go up and I knew Lauren would be miserable in her pants. I asked if she wanted my shorts and she did. There was no bathroom near the soccer field, so we awkwardly took off our bottoms in the back seat of the car and traded. When the game was over, Dave came over to the car to get us so we could walk over to the potluck together. When I exited the car in my too tight Lululemon pants, Dave looked at me and said, "Wow, those look rough."

I was well aware that my waistline was much bigger than Lauren's, but I wasn't exactly auditioning for the TLC show *My 600-lb Life* either. *Rough* was not a smart thing to say. I angrily stomped over to the family potluck, wearing my second-skin leggings, feeling slightly self-conscious (obviously I didn't eat anything) as I melted in the blazing sun. Clueless Dave couldn't understand why I was so angry; he thought his earlier observation was helpful. I guess it could have been helpful if I actually thought those sweaty, tight pants were figure-flattering and I had something else to wear.

After the potluck, we drove the three hours home in complete silence. Dave was too afraid to say a word and with good reason. Later in the evening, after several hours of icy silence, I explained to Dave that maybe next time he could say something like, "Did you switch bottoms with Lauren? That was so nice. I am so lucky to have such a selfless wife."

Missing most of Kelsey's college games was hard. I can never get those years back. But in hindsight, it probably helped save our marriage.

Although I was missing my graduation, I decided I should go ahead and order my cap and gown. It would be fun to wear while I cooked dinner.

Late that December, Lauren and I went back to Florida for a one-week refresher at the Aphasia Center. I had never been to the beach in December. The water was much too cold to swim (or to do aerobics) but every day I would sit in a beach chair soaking up the warm sun reflecting over the past few years. Our family had been through many changes. I was proud that no matter what life threw at us, we held ourselves together and continued to forge ahead. If it wasn't for our inappropriate sick sense of humor, we may have never survived. I was finally close to the point where I could laugh at something without feeling suffocating sadness at the same time. Mothers tend to carry the weight of the world on their shoulders and I am no exception. Someone once told me that a mother is as happy as her saddest kid. I hated that because it made me think, *wow, I have a lot of kids, someone is always bound to be sad; I'm doomed.*

But I wasn't doomed; I was blessed. And I was thankful that even though something terrible happened to us, we figured it out. Somehow, we all managed to keep it together and make things better.

I have heard of many examples where difficult situations tear marriages and families apart. I'm, thankful that wasn't us, and that Dave learned to keep his mouth shut when I looked bad in tight pants. We had many rough times, especially January of 2015 when I considered placing a pillow over his head. Dave most likely could say the same thing about me. I wasn't exactly a picnic. I would be lying if I said any of this was easy. Our time apart had been hard.

Ryan and Maggie like to refer to my time in Chicago and Omaha as "Remember that time when mom left us for months at a time?" They say it because they know it bothers me. Children learn by actions. All the years of watching me purposely pushing their dad's buttons to annoy him must have rubbed off on them.

———

While I was in Florida, the kids devised a plan to rent a local movie theater for a viewing of my documentary for family and friends. I was super proud of what I created but it was far from Hollywood material. My filming and editing skills were immensely basic. I didn't want to embarrass myself, or worse, embarrass my family. It was a hard sell for them to persuade me to share the movie with others. Shannon was the one who ultimately convinced me.

To say that the Murphy kids all have strong personalities would be a bit of an understatement. One of them (Erin) has more than one strong personality. When Erin was a teenager, I lovingly referred to her as "Sybil" (from the popular 1976 movie about multiple personalities starring Sally Field). With Erin, you never knew if you would get the super fun, creative Erin, the side-splitting hilarious comedian Erin, the crabby, sleepy, nap-taking Erin, or my personal favorite, the all-out raging lunatic Erin.

Thankfully, Shannon only had one personality. Unfortunately, her personality was to be brutally honest and bold ALL THE TIME. Now that they are older,

Erin is slightly less, psychotic, but Shannon has remained brutally honest and bold, maybe even more so. (She's still single.)

Shannon heard I was having reservations about inviting others to view the movie and called to convince me otherwise. "Mom, the movie is really good," she said. "You need to let us rent the movie theater."

I knew she of all people would give me an honest review. Then she followed up with "But . . . I did find one mistake that really bothered me. When you tell the story of Lauren recognizing Kris Jenner while watching *Keeping Up with the Kardashians*, you call her Kris Kardashian. You said it three times. Her name is not Kris Kardashian; it is Kris Jenner."

I should have known we couldn't end our conversation with a compliment. Sometimes I wish my kids weren't so afraid of me. "Fine, let's do it."

Lindsey's family also loved the idea of showing the film, we found a theater that held 160 people. Both families sent out invites over email and social media. Within two hours we had overbooked. I was beyond humbled. I didn't think anyone would want to see my little movie project. We decided to do two showings back-to-back in order to accommodate everyone. The next day our RSVP list had over 300 people and a growing waiting list. The movie theater did not have anything larger to offer us. I called Incarnate Word Academy, Maggie's high school, to see if we could use their theater and they graciously agreed.

The premiere was scheduled for January 3, which was also Ryan's nineteenth birthday. That morning I planned to take him to a celebratory lunch and then to the mall to pick out his birthday gift. I woke him up around 10:30 a.m. (my kids don't normally roll out of bed on Christmas break until late afternoon). It was going to be a busy morning. Before lunch, we needed to drive Lauren to her workout, swing by Office Depot to get the movie tickets printed, pick Lauren up, and *then* we could all go to lunch. Ryan was annoyed. He said he did not want to spend his nineteenth birthday with his mother running errands. I told him too bad and to get in the car. He pouted most of the morning.

Dave met us later at the restaurant for lunch. Ryan chose the place because they made his favorite strawberry ice cream cakes. When we ordered our food, I let the waitress know I also needed an ice cream cake to go. They were out of strawberry. Ryan looked at me like I ruined his life for the second time in one day.

We had just finished lunch when I noticed something wasn't right with Lauren. She couldn't get her words out. I swiftly reached in my purse and got her emergency seizure meds, placing one of the pills on her tongue. Dave told me later he felt I had a keener sense than a seizure dog. He and Ryan had no clue something was amiss. After the pill dissolved, we sat for five minutes or so until Lauren's speech improved, and she seemed more with it. Once I felt comfortable in her ability to walk, we settled the bill and headed to the parking lot. I planned to drop Lauren off at home for a nap before taking Ryan to the mall. Unfortunately this was something we were used to dealing with. When I pulled out of the parking lot, Lauren's eyes rolled back and I saw the dreaded eye blinks just before her head turned sharply and unnaturally to the right. I pulled into an empty parking lot across the street and called 911.

Her convulsions stopped as the ambulance was pulling up. I gave the paramedics a quick rundown of her history while they put her on a stretcher and checked her blood pressure and heart rate. As they moved her to the back of the ambulance she started seizing again. I knew this third seizure was going to warrant a trip to the ER. I looked at Ryan and said, "I'm sorry, buddy. I know this is a crappy birthday. Can you please drive my car home?"

This was the hardest part for Dave and me. It was bad enough that seizures and ambulances were part of our everyday life, but we hated it for our kids.

One time Lauren had a thirteen-minute seizure at home. It must have been a slow day in our city because after I called 911 it seemed as if the whole city showed up. A fire truck, an ambulance, and two or three police cars were all in front of our house. Before the cavalry arrived, I sat on the couch with Lauren as she continued to seize. I asked Ryan if he could grab my bra off the bathroom floor. (Why can't she have seizures when I have my bra on?) In a normal situation Ryan would look at me like I had three heads and tell me no, but he couldn't say no in this type of situation. He brought me my bra as if he was carrying poison, barely touching the strap with two of his fingers pinched together.

Moments later, our house was filled with first responders. I looked around the room at the scared looks on my kids' faces, and my heart hurt for them. It had been Lauren's longest seizure to date. Thirteen minutes in *seizure time* feels more like thirteen hours. The paramedic gave her a shot of Versed, which thankfully ended her convulsions. En route to the hospital, the police drove ahead of the ambulance and blocked off the roads to traffic. Our first responders never cease to amaze me.

Later that evening when Lauren was discharged, I told Maggie how much her dad and I hated for her and her siblings to witness the scary seizures. Maggie told me, "It wasn't completely terrible. Ryan and I were just saying how it's really nice when Lauren goes to the hospital after a seizure because you and Dad always feel so bad you bring us home food."

It seems as if my children have also learned to "find the positive."

After the *Happy Birthday Ryan seizure,* Lauren had blood and urine tests done at the hospital. They found no sign of infection. Many times we know what causes a seizure and sometimes seizures seem to come out of nowhere. This is unfortunately the nature of her injury. A few hours later, Lauren was back napping at home. We had very little time before setting up for the movie premiere. Ryan's birthday shopping spree would have to be rescheduled.

After the movie we had a reception with wine and cheese. It was great to hear such positive feedback, especially from the medical community. I was overwhelmed with the number of doctors, nurses, and therapists that came. There were also several TBI survivors in attendance, who were happy to see someone shine a bright light on brain injury awareness.

Lauren was still dealing with the negative side effects of her series of seizures the next morning. We opted for a nice quiet day. That evening, once Dave was at home to stay with Lauren, I took Ryan to the mall and because of my never-ending mom guilt, I spent triple the amount I was planning on spending. I still owe him a strawberry ice cream cake.

A few weeks later, Amanda, a professor from Fontbonne University who had been invited to my premiere by Lindsey's parents, asked if she could show my movie to their speech students and aphasia clients. I felt honored.

Lauren and I attended the viewing and were part of a discussion panel. Amanda asked if Lauren would be interested in joining their aphasia group two days a week. I agreed to bring her the next week to check it out. Lauren seemed to enjoy going to the clinic, plus it filled up her day and gave her something to look forward to. All of the aphasia clients, with the exception of Lauren, were stroke survivors. Lauren was the only TBI patient, and by far the youngest in their group. Lauren was benefiting from the clinic and was signed up to attend their upcoming summer boot camp.

I never stopped looking forward, always searching for the next step for Lauren. I had to do everything in my power to keep her from becoming stagnant in her recovery. My next adventure involved an aphasia cruise. Who knew something like this was out there? What could be more motivating than meeting other people with aphasia in the Caribbean? The rest of the Murphy kids didn't share in our enthusiasm, as they were not invited to join us. This wasn't a family vacation; it was part of piecing Lauren back together. She didn't need the distraction of all of her siblings, and I didn't need the expense. Besides, it gave them more to complain about ("Mom and Dad went on vacation and only brought their favorite kid.")

The aphasia cruise was put together by a nonprofit called Aphasia Recovery Connection (ARC). ARC was founded by a dynamic mother-son duo, Carol Dow-Richards and David Dow. David had a stroke at ten years old and has been spreading aphasia awareness for years. Because aphasia can be very isolating, ARC helps connect survivors, as well as caregivers, through social media, conferences, and cruises.

By the third night of the cruise, Carol enacted something she called the "David Rule." This rule was that the people with aphasia had to sit at a different table than their caregivers while at dinner. Before the David Rule, Dave and I inadvertently acted as Lauren's human shield; she always sat between us. There were around eighty people in our group and every single member knew the ins and outs of aphasia. Lauren did not need us to talk for her.

By the end of the week I could see Lauren's confidence emerging. The last night of the cruise was a New York-themed karaoke party. When we arrived in the conference room for that evening, Lauren was totally in her element. She stood front and center most of the night hogging the microphone. A few weeks later, Ryan came home from college for a visit and mentioned how amazing Lauren's speech and confidence had grown. The cruise really gave her a boost.

One of the things that attributed to Lauren's outer beauty before her accident was her confidence. Lauren would walk into a room and everyone noticed. She was a beautiful girl and always dressed well but the main reason she garnered so much attention was that she exuded confidence. She was remarkably bold and unafraid to speak with every single person in the room. Aphasia and brain injury stole that from her. It felt good to hear from Ryan that he could see a change, another sign Lauren was inching closer to recovery.

In September, the new semester at the Fontbonne's speech clinic began. Throughout the semester Lauren was able to take part in several aphasia awareness panels. The panelists had a list of ten questions and each person chose two or three questions that they wanted to answer. Lauren struggled with reading written responses. It was very difficult for me to sit in the audience and watch her difficulty responding. It helped that she wasn't the only one on the panel who had a hard time, as reading and writing is hard for many people with aphasia.

Lauren would shine during the Q&A portion. Although she still had moments of social inappropriateness, people often found her social gaffes refreshingly funny and I was learning that regardless of her deficits, Lauren still had an uncanny ability to win over a room full of people. While sitting in the audience observing, I could see Lauren come to life during her time in the spotlight. I hadn't seen her look so happy since before her accident. I knew that Lauren wouldn't ever be able to return to her old career, but I was determined to find a way to help her contribute to society in some sort of meaningful way.

Watching her light up during her Hall of Fame speech and the aphasia panel Q&A segments, I knew she was destined to share her story with others. It was my job to find a way. Her reading and writing and speech would need to keep improving. We would figure it out. Somehow, someway, she would get there.

Chapter Nineteen

THE FREAKS COME OUT AT NIGHT

I pride myself in always being strong and in control. With the exception of the first few weeks of Lauren's ICU days, I felt like I had a pretty good handle of things and knew what to do in order to keep moving Lauren as well as the rest of the Murphy family forward. One thing I wasn't prepared for was my brand-new habit of sleepwalking in a total crazed panic, also known as "Mom's night terrors."

The first time it happened I was in my apartment in Chicago. I had just fallen asleep after another long day shadowing Lauren's therapy. Sam and Erin were in town visiting and still awake watching TV in the living room. The buzzer on the dryer went off. I sprung from my bed and sprinted into the living room with a crazed look on my face. Sam and Erin asked, "Mom, are you okay?"

I stood there for a few seconds trying to process what was going on. Part of me knew I was dreaming and the other part of me was trying to find a way to help Lauren. When the dryer went off, my subconscious processed that it was Lauren's heart monitor. Somewhere in my mind I knew that Lauren was flatlining and I needed to save her.

Back when she was at Cedars in ICU she had a day where her heart rate plummeted. I sat in the corner of her room almost paralyzed as I watched her room fill with half a dozen nurses and doctors. They brought the crash cart and administered several doses of Epinephrine, commonly referred to as Epi. I watched the monitor signals continue to descend in the wrong direction. I was anxiously waiting for the Epi to kick in. When it didn't seem to be working, doctors made the decision to prepare Lauren's body for the paddles. To this day, the sound of someone peeling off any type of adhesive backing brings me right back to that scary moment. Lauren was still in a coma as they rolled her lifeless body over to apply the pads to her back and chest. I was frozen as I watched the numbers on the heart monitor go from the high thirties all the way down to the low twenties. I had never prayed with such desperation in my entire life. All of those prayers that I often recited on autopilot during my many years of Catholic school took on a whole new meaning. As Lauren's heart rate slowed down, mine was beating out of my chest. I couldn't lose her. I pleaded with God, with Jesus, with Mary, with the whole freaking communion of saints. *My God, no. Not my little girl. She has so much life ahead of her, I can't lose her, I just can't.*

I will never know if it was the power of prayer, the power of science, or both—and honestly, I don't even care which—but thankfully her heart rate began ascending, I watched the faces of everyone in the room begin to relax and eventually they wheeled the crash cart out into the hallway where it belonged. I remained frozen in my chair wondering what the heck just happened.

My best guess is that now that Lauren was in Chicago and her life was no longer in danger, my brain was finally processing everything that I had witnessed at Cedars. I eventually woke myself up enough to realize the sound was just the dryer buzzer. Sam and Erin had a good laugh as I walked back inside my bedroom and shut the door.

This was my first episode of unfortunately many more to come.

Ryan was the next victim of my night terrors. His bedroom is right next to mine and Dave's. One evening I bolted out of bed, ran to his doorway, and told him he needed to *push the button*. He was still awake and looked at me funny. "What button?" he asked.

I was completely frantic. Somehow, I believed that if Ryan didn't push this "button." he would die. The only problem was that I didn't even know where the button was or what it looked like. I stood there in a full out panic. I solely held the key to keeping my son alive and I couldn't even help him. What kind of mother was I? The button was nowhere to be found. "Ryan, push the button, please push the button!"

I woke up enough to realize I was living in an alternate state of consciousness. Ryan sat in his bed looking at me like, *Who is this crazy lady?*

Again, I offered no explanation, turned toward my room, and climbed back into bed. While I was still half asleep, I wondered if maybe there *was* a button, and I should go back in there and see if I could find it. These episodes were strange. Even after I was more awake, part of me felt as if they were real and I needed to act upon whatever task my subconscious was telling me to do or one of my kids would die.

My daughter Erin works in a pediatric ICU. She insists that it's a real issue for parents of kids in the ICU to have PTSD. I rolled my eyes and told her I was fine. I could not have PTSD, that was for people in combat. I wasn't worthy of having PTSD.

These episodes seemed to be more frequent during stressful times. When Lauren would have seizures the whole family knew to be on the lookout for their mom running around the house frantically searching for a way to keep everyone alive. One bad thing that happened as a result of my night terrors was that I clenched my teeth, causing my already less than perfect teeth (after years of braces) to resemble a picket fence.

Because of our sick sense of humor, my family often laughed at me as they watched me spout off crazy things in a state of panic. Maggie's bedroom was the furthest away from mine. She was thoroughly disappointed that she was the only one in the house who hadn't witnessed my semi-conscious sleepwalking firsthand. My family urged me to go to the doctor to get help, but I refused. What was I supposed to say? "I'm here because sometimes I'm crazy in my sleep?"

Taking sleeping pills wasn't an option. What if Lauren had a seizure? I would just have to find a way to deal with it on my own.

Courtney got to witness my crazy night terrors the first night we were in Orange County, California for their friend's wedding. Lauren and Courtney were in one bed and I was in the other. Before we went to sleep, Courtney realized that she forgot to pack pajamas. I brought an extra nightgown and gave it to her. The gown was covered in head-to-toe hot pink owls. Not exactly fashion forward, but it was super soft and comfortable. Courtney referred to it as a muumuu. I gently reminded her that I wasn't even fifty years old; I don't wear muumuus. It was a nightgown. Early that morning around 5:00 a.m., the fire alarm went off in the hotel. I bolted out of bed, ran to the door, ran into the bathroom, and frantically ran back toward the bed. I picked up the bedside phone and dialed the front desk. When they answered I said, "Hello, this is Colleen in room 432 and my daughter has a speech disorder called aphasia. Somehow she got confused and made the fire alarm go off. I'm so sorry, it is a false alarm."

He asked my room number again and said okay. I hung up the phone and the alarm immediately shut off. Courtney, now wide awake, looked at me and said, "What?"

I knew that I was still half-asleep and told her, "Give me a few minutes and I will be able to explain."

I sat in my bed for several minutes, trying to understand if I was awake or asleep. After a few minutes, I fell back asleep sitting up. I woke up to hearing heard Courtney say, "I am still waiting for you to explain."

I was now fully awake. I laughed when I told her I vaguely remembered calling the front desk and I must have been asleep when I did it. And not to worry, this happens all the time to me. Her next question was "So *is* the hotel on fire?"

That I couldn't answer. Courtney called down to the front desk to ask if there was a fire? They told her that the alarm went off due to the hot steam of someone's shower. It was just a crazy coincidence that the alarm stopped at the exact same time I took full responsibility for it. Courtney hung up and we were dying laughing. Lauren woke up and looked as us like we were crazy which just made us laugh even harder, she rolled over and went right back to sleep. This was the first time I involved an outside source in my crazy night terrors. Courtney told me she was just thankful she didn't have to evacuate the building wearing a muumuu. For the last time, it was a nightgown! I can only imagine what the guy at the front desk thought of my phone call. He played along with my craziness beautifully.

Sometimes I wake up and laugh after an episode and sometimes I am overcome with sadness. Most times I don't remember unless Dave or one of the kids ask me about it the next day. Four years after Lauren's accident I finally saw a doctor and she told me that yes, I was definitely showing signs of having PTSD.

I have come to terms with all of this just being another part of the journey. One thing that I can say I have learned over the last several years is that I have very little control over what happens. But what I can control is how I react. I choose to embrace my crazy and find the humor. I'm a pretty funny person but while I'm asleep I am freaking hilarious. One of my favorite sleepwalking stories was when I woke up thinking there was a hole in our bedroom floor. Dave was awake laying on the floor doing work on his computer. I jumped out of bed, ran over to my clean pile of laundry, and found the biggest t-shirt in the pile. I brought it to Dave and asked him to cover the hole in the floor so one of the kids didn't fall through it. Dave is learning to just "go with it." He told me he would take care of the hole as I climbed back into my cozy bed, satisfied that I saved my children from an untimely death. Covering the hole in the upstairs bedroom floor with one of my favorite V-neck tees was clearly the best way for the hole to be fixed.

Surviving trauma is a family affair. We have *all* lived with the effects for so long some of the crazy stuff is beginning to seem normal. Things that would have seemed crazy before the accident are now part of our everyday life. One of us driving to Walgreens at 8:30 p.m. because Lauren is down to three ChapSticks in her purse is a little crazy. Before her accident that would have been insane. Now we know that everyone will sleep better if Lauren feels she has enough ChapStick to keep her lips properly moisturized. Well, most everyone. I will most likely still be running around the house sleepwalking, trying to save the people I love from an untimely death.

Chapter Twenty

NOW WHAT?

We passed the five-year mark of Lauren's accident and were still work-ing tirelessly on improving Lauren's speech, reading and writing. Many days I wondered if we were spinning our wheels. Were things actually improving? Whenever those negative feelings would begin to surface someone would inevitably show up out of nowhere and tell me a story of how well Lauren communicated verbally with them since their last encounter. I was thankful for those types of moments. I needed those to feel refreshed and to continue moving forward. A positive attitude is one of the best things someone can do for an unfortunate situation, yet after five years I was getting tired of trying to remain positive.

Some days I just needed permission to be in a bad mood. I was bored with trying to fake happiness. Suzy Sunshine was drained, and sick of all the bull. I longed for my old life (that I previously thought was hard) and wished I had just one day without brain injury. I didn't mean I wanted a vacation, but instead I wanted a magic wand to make everything back to the way it was just for one day. Heck, I would settle for one hour. I was tired of feeling as if I was failing every single day. As Lauren's primary caregiver I felt her hardships or lack of progress were a direct result of me not doing enough to help her.

I read so many self-help books on living with brain injury and/or aphasia and none of those books mentioned the crazy or hard stuff. This reminded me of the contrast of my own flowery Facebook posts or family Christmas cards versus reality.

Every year we would try and come up with something clever to send out on the family Christmas card. I have threatened to cancel more times than I care to count. When the kids were little, I came up with the brilliant idea to do a card with all of the girls in robes with towels around their heads wearing green facial masks. Ryan would wear a towel around his waist and a shaving cream beard. What could go wrong? Maggie was around eighteen months and Ryan was close to four. This was before the luxury of digital cameras. I went through almost a whole roll of film just trying to get everyone to look in the same direction. The girls' faces were beginning to dry out and crack and Ryan's inability to sit still was causing his towel to continue to fall off and he was getting shaving cream in his mouth. Dave stood behind me as I snapped imperfect photos. Ryan kept whining about the taste of the shaving cream. I was normally the disciplinarian in our house, but I was too busy trying to get the perfect shot when I heard Dave tell Ryan, "Smile, you need to smile, right now, smile or get hit!"

With that I laughed and said, "Fa la la la la la la la la!" I may have been the craziest parent but at least I never threatened violence over a Christmas card.

Now that the kids are older, Dave calls each kid individually to stress how important the family Christmas card is to me and to please not be the one to *mess it up* this year! Through the years we have dealt with many snags during the infamous Murphy family photo shoot. It's not an official photo shoot unless at least one person is crying. Once, Erin stepped in dog poop, another time Kelsey stepped on Shannon's hair. Ryan farted on Sam's hand. And my personal favorite was when seventeen-year-old Shannon threw up during our photo shoot because she was so hung over.

Despite the painful process, every single year I send over one hundred photo cards showing my *big happy family*, color-coordinated and smiling at the camera. Only the people in the photo know the truth: they strongly disliked each other at the precise moment the picture was taken.

Lauren's Facebook recovery page was similar. It was full of Positive Polly posts highlighting all of her milestones and triumphs. I never posted about the times when Maggie would pick Lauren up from therapy only for Lauren to scream at and berate her the whole way home. If Maggie wouldn't change lanes the second Lauren told her to or if she felt she should drive faster or slower or maybe even stop at Walgreens because she was getting low on Kleenex, there was trouble. This was the ugly side of brain injury. We all understood *why* Lauren acted that way but that didn't make it any easier.

I was tired of pretending like everything was okay when it wasn't. One example was one of our first visits to the Aphasia Center in Florida. I was having a particularly bad day while Lauren was at therapy, so I went grocery shopping at Publix as a distraction. I remember pushing my cart down an aisle and when I came across the store manager. We made eye contact and he asked, "How are you today?"

I smiled at him and said, "I am fabulous, thanks for asking." As I continued down the aisle, I laughed at myself when I thought about what I *really* wanted to say: "Thank you so much for asking. Actually I am terrible. You see, a couple of years ago my daughter ran in front of a speeding car and everything changed. I have been stuck in this Godforsaken town feeling like I am in a monastery living with a monk because my daughter can no longer have a simple conversation with me. I came here today because I just ran out of ice cream. This morning I finished my twelfth carton because I miss my family and I am trying to eat my pain away."

That Publix trip made me think more about everyone else. Maybe that Publix manager was dealing with his own life crisis. Wouldn't it be wonderful if everyone walked around with their troubles written on a sign? Maybe the world would be a little kinder. I had a gazillion examples like that morning in Publix. Dave was the only one who knew how mentally exhausted I often felt. He was also the sorry sap who was on the receiving end of most of my bitterness.

On our second trip to Florida, I was sitting with Lauren explaining to her how important it was to continue to have goals. I asked her to think about what she wanted more than anything. I wasn't sure if she could understand what I was trying to tell her so I reworded it to try and make it simpler for her to understand. I asked, "What is the one thing you wish for the most?"

She walked toward the kitchen table, picked up her notebook, and wrote "God."

It took me a second to process how profound what she wrote actually was. What more could she need? Catholics are the worst at knowing Bible verses, but even most cradle Catholics can remember the Bible verse that says, "With God all things are possible."

She was absolutely right, and she was showing me that she already had the only thing that she needed. With God on her side she couldn't lose. Lauren has always had strong faith even during her Easter, Christmas, and Ash Wednesday-only churchgoing days. Whenever she heard of someone who needed prayers she would stop in at St. Patrick's Cathedral and light a candle. Following her quick pit stop at St. Patrick's, she would promptly let her mother know she went to church, even if going to church merely consisted of lighting a candle, saying a quick prayer, and heading out the door.

Goal setting has always been a big part of Lauren's drive and success. When she lived in New York, she set a goal to make $100K by the time she turned twenty-five. When that didn't happen, she changed the goal to sometime during her twenty-fifth birth year. As her mother, I felt her goal was insane and life isn't about the size of one's salary. She ultimately reached her goal after the accident with her salary combined with fundraisers and her GoFundMe account. I don't think that was what she had in mind when she set that high-reaching goal, but regardless, she reached it.

While we were on our aphasia cruise, I received a message from Courtney that a professor from Columbia University who stumbled upon the *Life of the Lucys* blog years ago, would like the two of them to come in and speak to her class about breaking though communication barriers with aphasia, and maintaining friendships. Lauren was looking forward to sharing her story and had been asking me if she could do more public speaking. I gave her a generic response: that of course she could; she could do anything she set her mind to. I wasn't exactly expecting anyone to ask her to speak so I felt it was safe to tell her that yes, that would be fun, and she would be great.

Her aphasia class at Fontbonne spent a good part of the opening weeks of the fall semester talking about the importance of goals. She and all of her aphasia classmates were asked to come up with a goal that they wanted to work on over the school year. Lauren had decided that she would like her goal to be becoming a better public speaker. Lauren's speech deficits would make public speaking a lofty goal. Leave it to Lauren to seek out a goal that was next to impossible. Did she remember that she is missing a section of her brain, the part that is responsible for sight and sound processing as well as language usage? I think it would have been a better goal to become an artist, or a ballet dancer, if only she could paint or dance. As her mother, I knew that I had to support her and more importantly believe in her ability to make this work. She wouldn't be able to do it alone and despite my inability to speak in front of a crowd- I knew that this new task would fall on me. Yippee!

While Lauren worked hard on regaining reading and writing skills, I tried to figure out how to design a website and come up with a logo for branding. If she was going to make a go at speaking in public, I would have to transform myself into her momager, just like Kris Kardashian . . . I mean *Jenner*.

It was important to at least look professional since her weakness would obviously be speaking.

Memorizing a presentation wasn't an option. Lauren's memory was comparable to Dori's in *Finding Nemo*. Reading off a paper wasn't an option either; she can only read short phrases. Once we got past "Good Morning" we might have a problem. Then I remembered a couple of my favorite quotes: "Fake it till you make it" and "If you throw enough crap at the wall, eventually, some of it will stick."

And my personal favorite: "Murphys Don't Quit."

We hired someone to help us with the website, designed a logo, opened Instagram and Twitter accounts, and ordered business cards. We were ready to launch the website at the end of November.

I wanted to have her website, Instagram, and Twitter accounts live before her trip to New York and speech at Columbia University. She already had several thousand followers on her Facebook page and I knew her followers would help spread the word. Most have been with her throughout her recovery journey.

I brought my tripod and camera equipment with me the day of Lauren's Columbia University speech. While I was setting up in the corner of the room, the students began to arrive. Lauren greeted each and every one with a smile and a handshake as she introduced herself. Shyness was never in her wheelhouse. She then stepped out of the room for a second so she could go over her index cards. She had a few phrases written down that she studied the whole time we were on the subway. Courtney would be doing the majority of the speaking, but Lauren had several parts sprinkled throughout the presentation.

The girls were standing in the front of the classroom ready to begin when Lauren started walking toward me in the back of the room. I was afraid that she was getting cold feet. I couldn't imagine what she was coming over to tell me when she said, "Mom, we are getting ready to start. Make sure you hit record."

She was in complete control and within moments she had won over the entire room. Her comedic timing was impeccable. The next day Courtney received an email from the professor telling her how much the students LOVED their presentation and that she finally had to kick them out of the classroom because they couldn't stop talking about how inspirational Lauren was and how special the two guests' friendship was to witness.

That night in the hotel I stayed up until two in the morning going over the footage from their talk and piecing together a promo video to share over social media. Up until that point I still had reservations as to whether or not speaking in public was something that Lauren was capable of doing. Watching her win over that classroom in a matter of minutes showed me that my daughter was still the same bold, bright, beautiful girl that she has always been despite her many challenges.

Once we were back home, I posted the photos and video clip from Columbia. It didn't take long before I had a few more leads for speaking engagements. Our next one was scheduled at a school for a faculty meeting the first week of January. I quickly got to work on putting together our presentation including a PowerPoint slideshow. Using the PowerPoint gave Lauren visual clues to what we were talking about and where we were in the presentation. Routine would need to be a priority. I also knew that we would need to take it slow and not expect too much. Hopefully we would get into a good rhythm and put something together that we could be proud of. Our target audience would be schools, rotary clubs, and church groups-basically, anyone who was willing to hear us speak, we would be there with bells on. Our goal was one speech per month. With each new notification and email, I realized Lauren was going to have a very busy and successful 2019.

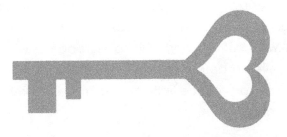

Key 5: Never Give Up

Many of us have experienced wanting to quit something at one time or another, but something or someone encouraged us to keep going. The key is to not wait for some type of sign from above; always believe in yourself, and NEVER give up!

Most mothers aren't given the opportunity to raise their children twice. I was. Seeing the milestones a second time has given me a greater appreciation for life and has left me in awe.

Had I listened to the doctors and therapists, Lauren's future could have been one of living in a long-term care facility, simply existing. Instead, she is thriving and captures the hearts and minds of everyone she comes in contact with. Never underestimate the power of the human spirit; keep moving forward, no matter how slow the progress. You got this!

When my kids were in preschool, the teacher only had two rules: *don't hurt* and *use words*. I saw them posted on the board at orientation, and I thought she needed a few more rules. Preschoolers can be challenging. When it was my turn to be the parent helper, I realized quickly I was wrong. Those simple rules were all that were needed. Everything applied, EVERYTHING!

The same could be said with the five keys Lauren and I have learned. Most of you reading this book won't have a catastrophic illness to deal with, but the road of life always comes with a few bumps and maybe even a detour or two. My wish is that whatever you are facing right now, or will face in the future, these five keys will bring you hope and comfort.

1. *Show Up*
2. *Find Your Cheerleader*
3. *Kindness is Free*
4. *Work Hard*
5. *Never Give Up*

One of my biggest takeaways throughout this journey is that I was never alone. I have always been a person of strong faith. Throughout the years, when life felt challenging, I often silently questioned whether or not God was real. Did all those years of Catholic school help me grow closer to God, or did it just brainwash me into believing something far-fetched and fictitious?

I can now answer with the strongest conviction ever: God is real and was absolutely with me every step of the way. He was the one holding my head up when my strength was gone. God was in that ICU room. I could feel him every step of the way.

Later in Lauren's recovery, when we would hit a plateau or when things seemed impossible to conquer, someone or something—an email or a phone call—would come out of nowhere and show me the way. I know in my heart those things weren't coincidental. Doubting Thomas has officially left the building.

Lauren's story is miraculous; although, it appeared as if I was in the driver's seat most of the time, I was never in charge of the wheel. I give all the glory to God.

Chapter Twenty-One

PUBLIC SPEAKER

D ave and I disagreed on the wording of Lauren's new business cards. When the proof came back from the printer, listed under her name was: *Public Speaker, Traumatic Brain Injury Survivor.*

Dave didn't feel we should put that she was a public speaker. He thought it was misleading. I, on the other hand, was completely confident it was only a matter of time before her speaking world tour would take off. Okay, maybe not completely confident, but *"fake it till you make it."* I never listen to Dave, so I went ahead and gave the printer the green light.

Before our first official speaking gig, Amanda from Fontbonne invited us to present in front of Lauren's aphasia class the day before, kind of like a dress rehearsal. By the time the date rolled around we had two more speeches scheduled, one for an office of mental health counselors and another for a group of third graders. The thought of presenting to third graders made me feel like *I* might need to receive services with the mental health counselors. Kids are brutally honest; I was fearful that I wouldn't be able to successfully gear the presentation toward that age group.

A snowstorm caused our "dress rehearsal" at Fontbonne to be canceled. The next day we muddled through our first official presentation. It was not exactly an Academy Award performance but Lauren's story is inspiring despite our amateur delivery. Amanda asked if we would still present to her group later in the week and we, of course, obliged. When we finished talking to Lauren's aphasia classmates we asked for questions or comments. One of the graduate students raised her hand and said, "I don't have a question, but I have a comment. Lauren you are absolutely incredible."

I knew then that Lauren's story was bigger than us and she was meant to share it.

Although I agree that her speaking in front of people is a good thing, one thing you will never hear me say is "Everything happens for a reason." Before Lauren's accident I was the type of person that might have said that to someone. Now that I know better, I think, *everything happens for a reason* is BS and if someone would say that to me, I would seriously contemplate punching them in the face. What reason could there be for my child to almost die and for years later still struggle for every single spoken word?

This is my public service announcement: Stop saying stupid crap to grieving people.

My list of things *not* to say to people in crisis is a mile long. One of my favorite questions that someone actually said to me was "Will she ever be normal?"

I wanted to respond, "I don't know, will you ever not be stupid?"

Instead it came out like, "We are hopeful for a full recovery."

I get it. People mean well, and many of them don't know any better. I am sure that I have said my fair share of stupid things to other people. I have spent most of my life with my foot in my mouth so I can be extremely forgiving when it comes to dumb statements. But what I really struggle with is the people who chose to say nothing. Tragic situations are hard to talk about, but when the people you hold dear and love the most in the world seem to disappear into the witness protection program while you are still figuring out how to just continue breathing, it makes it difficult. Saying something stupid is better than saying nothing. Don't assume your loved one knows you are thinking of them . . . TELL THEM!

Although I agree Lauren was meant to share her story, I don't feel that she was meant *for* her story. God gives us all free will. Unfortunately Lauren's free will brought her in the pathway of a speeding car. Her recovery and comeback are the reason her story should be shared. Her accident was tragic and awful, and nobody will ever convince me that there is a reason on this planet that could make any of it even slightly okay.

Brain damage is intense. Lauren has had an amazing comeback, but her recovery is far from over. She still needs me full time for support and may always need me. Lauren is also vulnerable to the outside world. Most people are loving, but every once in a while, we come across a real jerk. Once at a Cardinals baseball game Lauren was accused of being drunk. The guy behind her said something to her and her response didn't make any sense. I was too far away to hear what was going on, but Maggie told me later that the guy was mouthing off. I sat in my seat wondering how I should handle the situation. Part of me wanted to ask Dave to punch him in the face, but I knew Dave was too much of a Boy Scout and Fiona wasn't due to arrive for several hours. It would be best for me to handle the situation.

I waited until Lauren went to the bathroom with one of her siblings and then quietly approached the guy and let him know that not all disabilities were visible and people like him made outings with disabled family members troublesome. I could feel the ice building up in my veins. I wanted to unleash the most powerful venom-laced rant that I could muster. Instead, I offered him a warm smile and said, "Things aren't always what they appear to be. Kindness is free."

He sat there stunned; I turned and went back to my seat. A few minutes later, he left the game. "Kindness is free" is universal and Lauren and I now use that phrase in all of our speeches. Until I became a caregiver of a disabled child, I never realized how blind I had been to the disabled community. I never thought twice about using a handicapped bathroom stall, parking too close to the striped lines on a handicapped parking spot, or how hard it was for people in wheelchairs when the automatic door button is broken. Several times when Lauren was in a wheelchair, I would be forced to open a door and hold it with my toe as I awkwardly pushed Lauren's wheelchair through the doorway. These were all things that never occurred to me until I was the one needing help. Why are we programmed like that? If it doesn't affect us, it goes unnoticed. I quickly learned the world we live in was designed for the *abled* not the *dis*abled. We can do better!

Aphasia is common, yet 84 percent of people have never heard of it. More people have aphasia than cerebral palsy, Parkinson's disease, or muscular dystrophy. I was shocked when I learned those statistics. Before aphasia reared its ugly head in my family, I too was clueless. The awareness needs to change. So many people with aphasia live in solitude because going out into their communities is difficult. Lauren looks completely normal. Her mound of thick hair hides all the evidence of her four brain surgeries. But she's not "normal;" she struggles every day to live in a world that doesn't understand her.

———

After Lauren and I presented to her Fontbonne group, Amanda asked if we ever thought about speaking to a larger audience. I looked at Lauren and said, "Sure, we will speak to whomever will listen, right Laur?"

Lauren nodded in agreement.

What Amanda proposed next left me speechless, and I'm never speechless. She wanted to recommend Lauren and me for the spring commencement address. Without much thought we said we would love to. What were the chances that the school would actually choose someone who struggled with speaking to give the commencement address? That would be crazy.

Our presentation needed a lot of work. Up until that point, I was doing most of the talking, partly because Lauren has no memory of her accident (or the two years that followed) and partly because she struggled with speaking fluently. For us to do the commencement, I would need to shift the bulk of the speaking to Lauren. But how? I figured we would cross that bridge when we came to it. *If* we came to it.

First we had to get past the third graders. I needed to make some changes to our PowerPoint because the pictures from the first few days at Cedars were too gruesome for children. I found a cute drawing of a girl in pigtails with a head bandage, which would be a much more pleasant visual.

The day we spoke to the third-grade classes they were celebrating Pajama Day. How could we be intimidated by a group of kids wearing pajamas?

During our presentation I asked the kids to tell me some things that *they* could do to help others that doesn't cost money. (Remember, kindness is free.) With kids, you never know what type of answers you will get, or if they are even paying attention, but this group was very interactive and had great answers.

When we finished, there was time for Q&A. One kid asked how many stitches Lauren had. Another asked how long it took me to get to the hospital. And my favorite question was from a little boy who asked if Lauren had any pieces of the car stuck in her brain. Lauren and I both laughed. We knew that at least he paid attention.

———

With each speech, our delivery and Lauren's confidence improved. Thankfully, Lauren no longer told strangers that she loved them, but social skills were still an issue. Her behavior was often on the strange side. I tried to come up with a plan that would help to subtly correct her in public so she wouldn't feel like a chastised child. I used a hand signal or a facial expression that told her to stop what she was doing and redirect her behavior. One of the phrases I used with her was "Read the room."

I recommended that she look around her environment and try to mimic the behaviors of those around her. She still struggled with reading the room—simple things like grabbing her purse and coat before anyone else is leaving, or grooming lint or stray hairs off someone's sweater (doesn't matter if she knows them or not). My subtle hand signals would work well if she wouldn't roll her eyes and rudely (and loudly) say, "*Okay, Mom.*"

Reteaching social skills has been extremely difficult. Lauren has always had an aggressive personality, which I credit much of her recovery to, but when she offers someone some of her French fries and they say no, she aggressively tells them to eat some over and over again until they uncomfortably take a couple. Now we have a new phrase. There's not only "Read the room," but also "Too aggressive."

We are also working on not saying negative things in public. Lauren often announces, "No one will ever love me," "I can't drive a car," or "I still live with my parents."

My responses are normally the same. "You never know what your future holds. If you continue to work on your behavior and your speech you may be able to someday find love again. Work hard and believe in yourself."

As far as driving, I remind her that she was a terrible driver *before* the accident and the roads are much safer without her. Post-accident, Erin once let her drive home from a park near our house on New Year's Day. Dave and I had a mini heart attack when they told us. Lauren was pretty proud of herself. Turns out neither of them had a valid driver's license. Erin forgot to renew her license and had been driving around with her passport. Her fiancé had to explain that a passport was not a valid driver's license. Thankfully she's a pretty girl because obviously she's an idiot! An idiot who let her sister with a brain injury drive a car.

As far as Lauren complaining about still living with her parents, my response is to tell her how awesome her parents are. Plus she stole our bedroom. There was a scene in the movie *Mean Girls* where the character Regina George talks about making her parents switch bedrooms with her. I watched that movie with Lauren when she was in high school and she asked, "Can *we* switch bedrooms?" I laughed and told her of course not. Little did I know that almost ten years later she would be taking the master suite.

In some ways I felt that trying to re-direct and re-teach Lauren's behavior was the hardest part, maybe because that is the part that we are currently living in. Six years ago I would have given anything for Lauren to force-feed an acquaintance French fries or groom the lady next to her in church like a monkey. I have to remind myself that she has extensive brain damage and that often times I am expecting too much. For now, I am trying not to sweat the small stuff. Who cares if her purse needs its own chair at restaurants and that she goes into full panic mode when the W on the Walgreens sign on the outside of the building is burnt out.

A few years back on one of my flight home from Omaha, I was reading a brain injury-themed edition of *Chicken Soup for the Soul*. Halfway through I wanted to throw the book across the airplane cabin. Most of the stories were written by the survivors themselves. I hated it because Lauren still couldn't read or write or even tell her story. Brain injury has a pretty broad spectrum. There are mild traumatic brain injuries and severe traumatic brain injuries. In my opinion, many of the stories I read fell somewhere in between mild and severe. Nothing I read came remotely close to the severity of Lauren's injury.

And then I had an epiphany. The reason there weren't any stories of survivors of as severe as Lauren's injury was because there were *rarely survivors*, and those that did survive, often lived in a semi-vegetative state.

Once again, I felt like an ungrateful troll. Why did I struggle so often in understanding what a gift I had in Lauren? Every day she works so hard to do things that most of us take for granted. Who cares if she needs to have fifty Kleenexes and six ChapSticks in her purse to feel secure? Why do I continue to fight those things?

Shortly after our original conversation about commencement, Amanda let us know that the president of Fontbonne was on board and asking for board approval. Once that came through, Lauren would be the official 2019 commencement address speaker. Never in my wildest dreams when I launched her website could I have imagined we would be speaking at such a large venue so quickly. A few days later it was official—Lauren would be speaking to thousands of people. I had no idea what we were going to say or how we would pull this off.

For Christmas that year, we gifted Lauren a trip to Waco, Texas in May to run the Chip and Joanna 5K. Now I had to make the tough decision to cancel the trip because the race was only a week before the commencement address, and with Lauren's history of seizures while running, I felt it was too risky.

Back in November, we had transitioned medications again, and during the transition Lauren had a small breakthrough seizure two days before Thanksgiving. She was signed up for the Turkey Trot 5K on Thanksgiving morning. I told her I didn't think it would be a good idea to run two days after seizure activity. She didn't feel the same way (neither did Dave) and ran the race. Crowded races are always tough for her at the start line because maneuvering through a crowd is particularly hard. Dave normally has to verbally guide her through openings in the pack of runners. This was the first race she would be running on her new medication. Her ability to find her own way through the pack was a welcome change. The side effects from her previous medication kept her in a fog, despite her earlier break through seizure, we realized the medication change was long overdue.

I nervously waited for her at the finish line, spending the next thirty-three minutes praying silent Hail Marys.

Lauren was all smiles at the finish. I was thankful I didn't let my reservations or helicopter parenting stand in her way.

Since Lauren's accident she has finished over thirty 5K races. Dave is always with her and many times one of her siblings will join them as well. One time she even crossed the finish line while having seizure activity. On that particular race, Lauren's first two miles were faster than usual. With less than a half a mile to go, she started leaning to the right and her speech was becoming gibberish. A friend of ours passed Lauren and Dave on the course and Dave asked her to run ahead and let me know so I could have Lauren's emergency anti-seizure meds ready at the finish. When I saw them on the course walking toward me, I ran to them with the medication, telling Dave to move her to the grass and sit her down.

"We are going to cross the finish line first," he said. "We are only ten yards away."

For the next ninety seconds I walked alongside the course screaming at Dave to "Sit her down!"

We were quite the sight. He pointed to his blue bracelet. Was he seriously pulling the Murphys Don't Quit card? He ignored me and they forged ahead. I stood there screaming at him the whole way. Once across the finish line, Dave helped Lauren sit down on the grass. My screaming had already drawn a small crowd. I put the medication on her tongue and tried cooling her body down with wet towels. A few minutes later her convulsions began. I called 911 and Lauren left the park in the back of an ambulance, covered in wet towels and proudly wearing her finisher medal.

There would be no Chip and Joanna race this year, no discussion. I was putting my foot down. Lauren needed to be healthy for commencement. She was going to be mad, but she would get over it. This wouldn't be the first time she was mad at me and it sure as heck wouldn't be the last.

Even though our inbox was beginning to blow up with speaking requests, my plan was to not accept any offers in the month of April. Our normal presentation wouldn't work for commencement and I knew that Lauren would struggle with practicing two different presentations and could confuse the two.

My mind swam with thoughts and ideas. I had to come up with a speech that would resonate with our audience and, more importantly, I had to find a way for Lauren to do most of the talking. I began to regret our decision to do this. Lauren had no reservations and was excited. If we failed, we failed in front of *three thousand people*. Failing wasn't an option. I basically needed a miracle for her to pull this off.

One thing that I was definitely looking forward to after commencement was telling Dave I was right in regard to putting *Public Speaker* on Lauren's business cards.

Chapter Twenty-Two

SHE'S GOT THIS

Lauren and I got right to work trying to write our speech. During one of our many trial and error practice runs, I discovered that if I changed the presentation in any way, Lauren had a hard time remembering her lines. The format of our speech was more like a conversation instead of a prepared speech (a very scripted conversation). Typically, I would tell our audience parts of Lauren's story and then stop and ask Lauren specific questions to keep her involved and engaged.

One of the questions I ask is "How many brain surgeries did you have?" The answer is four. During one of our practice runs I accidentally skipped that question. Once I realized my mistake, I circled back and asked Lauren how many brain surgeries she has had. Her answer was "Plastic." This proved that Lauren needed everything in the same order every time.

Aphasia is frustrating. Even after almost six years, I still had a hard time understanding how Lauren couldn't answer a simple question. We had been working on fine-tuning our speech for weeks. I felt like I was beating my head against a brick wall. We couldn't even get past our opening line: "Congratulations class of 2019."

Rarely did she hit the mark. For whatever reason, Lauren kept saying, "Congratulations class of 2010."

I knew that if Lauren blew the opening line, we were doomed. I was beginning to lose patience, which in turn made me feel like a horrible human. Her speech deficits were out of her control.

I couldn't control how well Lauren remembered her portion, but I knew that the one thing I could control was the quality of our PowerPoint and content. The only problem was that I still had no idea what I was doing. The only applicable skill I felt I had was that I was a Murphy, and *Murphys don't quit.* I had to find a way for Lauren to win over a whole arena full of people, but how?

I sat through plenty of college graduations and couldn't remember a single commencement address. Nothing stood out to me. Then I thought, *What if one of them would have referenced the wrong year?* That I would have most likely remembered. Our speech would definitely be different than the average commencement address. One thing that I knew was that I had to make the speech more about the graduates, and less about Lauren.

In the meantime, my inbox was continuing to blow up with speaking requests. One afternoon we received a request to speak to over five hundred people at a college and within the same hour came a media request from a local TV show, *The Thread.*

It was still so unbelievable. Only a few months earlier I was trying to fake my way through a website design and now we were getting real-life media requests. The producer of the TV show asked if a camera crew could come and tape one of our presentations. I had to get permission from the elementary school where we were scheduled to speak in March before I gave the TV show the green light. A few days later, we not only received permission for the camera crew but another media request. A reporter from the St. Louis Archdiocese's newspaper, *St. Louis Review*, contacted me to see if they could send a reporter and photojournalist to the school on the same day. I secretly wondered if this would be the end of our speaking career, once they figured out we didn't know what we were doing.

Turns out, it was just the beginning. When Lauren speaks, people hang on her every word, even when it doesn't make a lick of sense. Audiences love her spirit and her funny personality. The article in the *St. Louis Review* was published a few days later. They did an amazing job telling Lauren's story.

Later in the week, the TV show's host came to our house to interview Lauren for the segment. When he arrived, Lauren wanted to show him something in her room. I thought she was bringing him in to see her running medals. Instead, she wanted to show him her list of goals that she taped to her wall. He was taken aback to see that Lauren is always looking forward. She realizes the past is the past, and she strives to always be better. Even with severe brain damage, Lauren understands life better than most of us, *including her own mother.*

Lauren's TV episode was set to air April 20, the Saturday morning before Easter, one day after the six-year anniversary of her accident. Every year I put together a recovery video. I decided the year before that the five-year video would be my last one. These videos were a ton of work. I had given the TV show access to all of our old photos and videos on my Google Drive. After seeing all of the old footage again, I couldn't let another year pass without somehow acknowledging her continued fight. I put together a quick, Flipagram-type video with several photographs. I posted the new video to her Facebook page on April 19. By the next morning, I had messages on both Lauren's Facebook recovery page and my personal page from our local news station, who had seen the video and were trying to reach me to do a story about Lauren's recovery.

That morning, her segment from *The Thread* aired and now we were talking with a journalist who wanted to tell Lauren's story on the 10:00 p.m. news. Was this real life? Lauren was loving all of this newfound attention, and I was beyond humbled.

Opening ourselves up to media coverage was risky. The media had complete control on what they put in the segment and not all of the footage was flattering. With both media outlets, *The Thread* and the local NBC affiliate, they had plenty of footage that showcased Lauren's deficits and her inability to understand some of the interview questions. Thankfully both media outlets shared beautiful renditions of Lauren's story.

The following week, we had our last scheduled presentation before her commencement address. The school was in Jefferson City (or Jeff City as we call it in Missouri). A reporter from their local newspaper, *The News Tribune*, came to hear us speak and ran a fabulous article a few days later. Lauren continued enjoying all the extra attention. With each new interview, her tenacity grew, and she held her had a little bit higher.

With our last scheduled speaking engagement behind us, we were able to focus solely on the commencement. Lauren knew how important it was to practice, practice, practice. Amanda gave me some great advice that really helped calm my anxiety. "If the speech is perfect," she said, "it won't be inspirational."

Wow, why didn't I think of that? She was absolutely right. Amanda didn't recommend Lauren for commencement because of her uncanny ability to speak in public; she was selected for her ability to keep trying in the face of adversity.

Being flawless was no longer my goal. We would do *our best* to prepare, knowing that perfection was not our main objective. Lauren and I did our speech a minimum of three times per day. Each practice was recorded and we listened immediately afterward to determine what worked well and what could be improved. While riding in the car, we listened over the radio on Bluetooth. Lauren's brain was completely immersed in her commencement address for several hours each and every day.

A few weeks before graduation, I had to fill out a form requesting our academic regalia. All members of the board and speakers were to wear a cap and gown at the ceremony. The form asked our field of study and level of degree. There were several options to choose from: AA, B.A., M.A., Ph.D. etc. I was extraordinarily grateful that instead of killing Dave in his sleep, I made the decision to go back to school to earn my degree. Mainly because I didn't see an option for *pregnant high school dropout* or *cosmetology license.*

The week before commencement, I received an email that a reporter from the *St. Louis Post-Dispatch* wanted to interview Lauren. The reporter came out to our house and asked Lauren several questions. Lauren was able to understand and answer some of the questions on her own; others required a little help from me. The reporter mentioned that she had previously learned of Lauren's story through social media. She had been personally following Lauren's progress for a long time and was excited to write the article.

It still baffles and amazes me that Lauren's story has touched so many people. What an honor it is for me to have a child that has touched so many hearts.

The faculty member in charge of operations for graduation requested us to meet him along with the technical guy at Chaifetz Arena a few days before commencement. They asked me to bring along our script, which would make it easier to know when the slides needed to advance. The only problem with that is that because of the unpredictability of Lauren, I often changed things on the fly. This is where my lifelong ability to fly by the seat of my pants comes in handy.

Unfortunately not everyone shared my passion and confidence for faking my way through the presentation.

While in the sound booth, they queued up our PowerPoint. We walked into the arena so Lauren could get the feel of the space. I got goose bumps when I walked into that huge stadium; all three giant screens displayed Lauren's photo above the words "*Lauren Murphy, TBI survivor, Aphasia Fighter, Motivational and Fitness Enthusiast, Runner, Inspirational Champion.*" The picture was taken on a recent trip back to New York City, under one of the many beautiful arched bridges in Central Park. Lauren was unquestionably radiant in her happy place.

I held back tears.

Lauren looked around the auditorium with a huge smile across her face. Six years prior, I was at Lauren's hospital bedside asking for God to grant me the impossible. In a few days Lauren would be showing thousands of people that *anything* is possible.

———

Lauren was as ready as she would ever be. At the urging of her stage mother, she spent over six weeks enduring constant repetitive practice. Lauren knew the material, and on every third our fourth practice run, everything came together. I wished I had more time to figure out how to help her be more consistent. My own performance and delivery were still far from perfect too. Public speaking was not something that had ever been on my bucket list. Regardless, I was confident we could do this.

Commencement was scheduled for four in the afternoon. There couldn't have been a worse possible time for Lauren. I knew that Lauren would be too excited to nap, and without a nap she would have late afternoon brain fatigue. Strategies were my normal go-to to combat a challenging situation for Lauren, but I was fresh out of workaround strategies for this one. Instead, I decided to take a play from the pre-accident Lauren Murphy playbook . . . *fake our way through it* and hope for the best.

The *Post-Dispatch* article came out the morning of the commencement and Lauren made the front page. Dave and I were shocked—the front page of the freaking *St. Louis Post-Dispatch*, this was huge! The headline read: FINDING HER VOICE: FONTBONNE GRAD GIVES COMMENCEMENT SPEECH AFTER TRAUMATIC BRAIN INJURY.

I felt like Lauren was finally catching a break. She spent years trying to regain so many things, simple things that most people take for granted. Her confidence was turned up yet another notch with the article's release.

That morning I scheduled blowouts for Lauren and me. (Some things never change.) Good hair was imperative in my opinion for a successful speech. Plus, I was hoping she would feel sleepy after getting her hair done. If I could have Lauren sneak in a twenty-minute nap, it could potentially make her afternoon more successful.

When we arrived home, we practiced a few more times. By then I was positively tired of our script, and so was Lauren. We needed to be at Chaifetz Arena around 2:30 p.m. I lied to Lauren and told her we had to be there at 3:30 p.m., which gave her plenty of time for a nap. I had drunk too much coffee that morning which only enhanced my jitters. While Lauren was sleeping, I was nervously upstairs throwing up.

Hours earlier at breakfast, Maggie was also a bundle of nerves. One of her sisters asked why *she* was so nervous and Maggie told her it was because she had seen us practicing. The others would ask how things were going. Many times I would say *fine,* the most overused BS word in the English language. Does "fine" ever really mean fine? Maggie knew the truth. Giving a commencement address with a severe language disorder was an extremely dumb idea.

We arrived on time and found our way to the stage for one last practice. Lauren had a strong run through. She seemed poised and confident. I was a bundle of nerves. We waited in a room downstairs with the board members who would be with us on the stage. Lauren and I would walk out at the end of the procession after all the graduates and faculty.

The last time I was in a cap and gown I was cooking dinner. Now here I was soon to be walking out to "Pomp and Circumstance." I carried my iPad and Lauren's handwritten index cards. As soon as my foot crossed over the threshold of the arena, and I could hear the music, I was holding back tears. So many emotions ran through my head. We were moments away from speaking to a crowd of over three thousand people. I spotted our family sitting together in a roped-off, reserved section and blew them a kiss as we made our way to seats on the center of the stage.

The minute I sat down, I knew I had to switch gears, calm my nerves, and focus on being strong and confident. Lauren needed me, and I refused to let her down.

During the introduction, the president of the university gave a condensed version of Lauren's accident and recovery. This was helpful because the audience then knew of Lauren's speech deficits before she approached the podium. Prior to the start of our speech, Lauren received an honorary doctorate. She beamed as the university president introduced her to the crowd as Dr. Lauren Murphy.

This was it.

We approached the podium. First I set up the iPad, which had our Power-Point show ready to go in presenter's view (seeing which slide was next was beneficial for me to remain on script). Lauren would be using the microphone attached to the podium. Mine was handheld and would go live when the control room saw me pick it up. Lauren was positively radiant and began with complete confidence and poise. She nailed her first line: *"Congratulations class of 2019."*

Thanks to YouTube it was easy for me to research past commencement speakers. I was able to go back several years to investigate. One thing I noticed was that each and every speaker thanked the president as well as the board members before their speech began. I knew that Lauren wouldn't be able to do that without butchering or forgetting names. I had to make a decision. Did I want to be the person to do all the thank-yous at the beginning? This was her speech, not mine. Did the graduates care about protocol? I decided to scratch the standard opening; Lauren was far from standard.

Standing next to Lauren and looking out at the sea of people, I couldn't help but notice she was able to grab everyone's attention from the get-go. The room was silent, the audience completely captivated. Lauren had a little mess-up on her second or third line ("What I was taught here at Fontbonne helped me become independent and strong" became "What I was taught here helped me become independent and *stressed*"). I quickly corrected her, which made the timing of the next line (mine) delayed. I was to mention that her independence brought her to New York with two suitcases and a big dream. When I didn't hit my mark, Lauren continued on without me. Once again, she was in complete control. The fact that she moved to New York was already mentioned in the intro. The audience had no clue anything was amiss.

Lauren's universal message to the graduates was the five lessons she learned on her road to recovery:

1. *Show Up*
2. *Find Your Cheerleader*
3. *Kindness Is Free*
4. *Work Hard*
5. *Never Give Up*

When Lauren expanded on "Find Your Cheerleader," we shared a video clip of one of her speech therapists cheering her on as she was trying to relearn to swallow. On-screen, she looked terrible. She was sitting in her multicolored neon wheelchair, wearing her hot pink skeletal pajamas, with a vacant look in her eyes. She couldn't even hold her shaved head up without help. Her speech therapist could be heard on the clip offering encouragement. The video footage was a stark contrast to the beautiful confident woman standing center stage with perfect hair.

We also showed a clip of Lauren trying to come up with Kelsey's name. The video was filmed a year and a half after her accident. It took over a minute for her to eventually say her sister's name. Lauren used many tools to assist her—photo flashcards, a notebook to write some of the letters, and verbal cues from me. The clip gave the viewers a true example of the struggle and complexity of aphasia.

Despite the disheartening nature of both clips, we were able to keep the tone upbeat with the playful banter of our well-rehearsed delivery.

Lauren figured out early into her speech that she had already won over the crowd. This gave her a bigger boost in confidence. I knew this would also cause her to go *off script*. She was feeding off the energy in the room and there was no stopping her. She was having a blast and it showed. On three different occasions during the speech she garnered huge bouts of applause. She also evoked several bursts of laughter with her ad-libs. The audience loved her, and she loved them.

Her speech ended with a recap of her five life lessons. She listed them once more with forceful conviction then closed with, "You got this class of 2019. You got this. Thank you!"

I watched in total awe as over three thousand people quickly rose to their feet applauding wildly. In just under fifteen minutes, she taught thousands of people life lessons that they will never forget. There is no denying her story is tragic; nevertheless she has found a way to turn her own personal tragedy into a positive way to publicly influence others. Had this been someone else's daughter up there speaking, I might have thought to myself, and wholeheartedly believed, that everything happens for a reason, because she has certainly found her destiny.

LET'S KEEP IN TOUCH

If you are new to our story and randomly picked up my book, I would like to invite you to continue with us on our journey. Lauren's story is far from over.

For our faithful followers that I like to refer to as "Team Murphy," thank you! Every single one of you can claim a piece of Lauren's success. Your messages, tweets, retweets, likes, comments, shares, and emails help Lauren and me remain positive, even on the toughest of days.

I read and return every single email.

If you would like to become part of Team Murphy, subscribe to murphysdontquit.com for frequent updates and inspiration.

We can be found on Facebook on the Lauren Murphy Recovery Page and on Instagram, Twitter, and YouTube @murphysdontquit and our website, murphysdontquit.com. If you are looking for resources for brain injury or aphasia, they can be found in the resources tab on murphysdontquit.com.

If you have a loved one battling a life-altering situation, I hope our story brought you a laugh or two, as well as comfort and hope.

ABOUT THE AUTHOR

Colleen Murphy is a wife, mother of seven, author, and public speaker.

In 2013, tragedy struck Colleen's family when her second oldest daughter, Lauren, was hit by a car and suffered severe brain damage. Colleen's main focus became helping piece Lauren back together again. With the help of specialists from all over the country, her family and friends, as well as her strong faith, she was able to do just that.

Today, Colleen and Lauren speak together as a team, inspiring thousands of people by sharing the details of Lauren's tragic accident, never-give-up attitude, and miraculous recovery. Colleen lives just outside of St. Louis, Missouri with her husband Dave. She spends her free time fielding countless phone calls from her children as they deal with the challenges of adulting and assisting her husband via FaceTime as he struggles to find things at the grocery store.

A free ebook edition is available with the purchase of this book.

To claim your free ebook edition:

1. Visit MorganJamesBOGO.com
2. Sign your name CLEARLY in the space
3. Complete the form and submit a photo of the entire copyright page
4. You or your friend can download the ebook to your preferred device

Morgan James
BOGO™

A **FREE** ebook edition is available for you or a friend with the purchase of this print book.

CLEARLY SIGN YOUR NAME ABOVE

Instructions to claim your free ebook edition:
1. Visit MorganJamesBOGO.com
2. Sign your name CLEARLY in the space above
3. Complete the form and submit a photo of this entire page
4. You or your friend can download the ebook to your preferred device

Print & Digital Together Forever.

Snap a photo

Free ebook

Read anywhere